ILLUMINATING

THE DARKNESS

The Mystery of Spook Lights

BY DALE KACZMAREK

- A Ghost Research Society Press Publication -

Books by Dale Kaczmarek
Windy City Ghosts (2000)
Windy City Ghosts II (2001)
Field Guide to Spirit Photography (2002)
Illuminating the Darkness (2003)

Original Cover Artwork Designed by
Larry E. Arnold (author of "Ablaze")
Visit www.ParaScience.com

This Book is Published by
- Ghost Research Society Press -
A Division of Ghost Research Society
PO Box 205 - Oak Lawn - Illinois - 60454
(708)425-5163
Visit us on the Internet at www.ghostresearch.org

First Printing - March 2003
ISBN: 0-9766072-5-5

Printed in the United States of America

Table of Contents

FOREWORD

Mysterious ball of lights have been reported for hundreds, if not thousands of years from all corners of the world. These strange lights have been called 'Spooklights', 'Ghostlights', earthlights, nim-nim lights, mystery lights, cemetery lights, or nocturnal lights and have been seen by people from all walks of life including: police chiefs, newspaper reporters, clergy, businessmen, farmers, and even the common man. Understanding the cause and source of these mysterious lights is another thing.

Overseas countries have their fair share of strange lights and have their own distinctive names for the anomalies. In Wales, an eerie spherical light that appears over the homes of Welsh families is always an omen of death and are called Tanwedd. The *canhywallan cyrth*, or corpse candle, is perhaps the best-known of Welsh phantoms. These strange lights are called candles because their shapes resemble that of a candle flame, and they also said to appear in the vicinity of a house just before someone is supposed to die.

Quinns Light is a phenomena reported in Australia and appears as a phosphorescent light about the size of a large bird, and goes round and round in circles before disappearing. Min-min lights is a term used for earth lights in Australia, especially ones on Aboriginal lands. It comes from the name of the hotel where they were first observed by white men and flits about Alexandria Station, the world's largest ranch covering 11,000 square miles. They are white in color and about the size of auto headlamps.

Paul Devereux in his excellent book entitled *Earth Lights Revelation* put together perhaps the largest collection of synonyms for earth lights anywhere in existence. The list includes: *Earth lights, Spooklights, Ghost lights, Mystery lights, Nocturnal lights, Nim-nim lights, Cemetery lights, Treasure lights, Night suns, Foo fighters, Fiery dragons, Luminous vapors, Fiery coruscations, Burning shields, Fiery drakes, Devil's bonfires, Amber gamblers, Strange lightning, Mysterious flares, Ghostly lanterns, Bodhisattva lights, ORBS, Strange meteors, Fluffy fire, Unctuous vapor, Blazing stars, Phantom effluence, Luminous columns, Ghost beacons, Luminous clouds, Flying flame,*

Sparkling fires, Flaming torch, Money lights, ALP, Geophysical meteors, Ghost Beacon, Elf-fire, Ghostly lights, Rocket lightning, Fireballs, Earthquake lights, Will-o'-the-wisps, Ignis fatuus, Fox fire, Fata morgana, Foolish fire, Fairy lights, Corpse candles, Elf light, Will-with-the-wisp, Wisp, Friar's lantern, Meg of the lantern, The swamp ghost, Bramaracokh, Peggy with the lantern, Fairy death lantern, Jack-o'-lantern, Peg-a-lantern, Flickering fire, Spunkie, Death light, Walking fire, Fools fire, Lambent flame, Fetch lights, Dead man's candles, Walking fire, Fair maid of Ireland, Friar Rush with a lantern, Ball of wildfire, Going fire, Fire of destiny, Robin Good-fellow, Hob-lantern, Fairy-lantern, Puck-lantern, Corpse light, Corposant, Corpo Santos, Dickepoten, Teine sionnii, Teine side, Fairy fire, Sean na gealaige, Jack of the bright light, Laim na lasoige, William with the little light, Feu follet, Irrlicht, Blud, Eskuddit', and Fetch Candle.

I will attempt to explain some of the better known above examples in the pages to come. Will-o'-the-wisps are small sources of light usually seen on swamps, marshes, mires or in deep woodland. They are different than earth lights in that they are usually small and no brighter than a torch. They are almost always extremely close to the ground as well (not going more than about ten feet in the air). They were feared in medieval times because they often led travelers astray, as the follower would believe they were town lights, or lights of a rescue party. These lights have led to the phrase "being pixie-led" and "fairy lights", as it was often believed that they were mischievous fairies or pixies. They are sometimes found on cliffs as well, luring ships to their doom. These lights are almost always blue, for reasons unknown. They are heavily described in folklore not just for their 'mischievous properties', but for their mineral locating abilities as well. Miners in Cornwall, England and the peak district believed that coal, silver and especially copper could be located by the presence of a blue vapor above the site where they are to be found. This was believed up until about the 19th Century, possibly even hanging on in the earlier parts of the 20th Century. A good example of this fact can be observed in Bram Stoker's book *Dracula*. Dracula is seen to be locating something at the beginning of the book by blue vapors.

The most common explanation for will-o'-the-wisps has always been ignited marsh gas, i.e. methane or phosphine. However, this has been disproved in every modern experiment because these gases both produce a hot yellow flame whereas will-o'-the-wisps are usually blue and cold. This points to a different type of chemical reaction, possibly the same type as used in bioluminescence. Will-o'-the-wisps will always be closely associated with earth lights, but aren't strictly the same thing. Certain fungi usually mentioned with will-o'-the-wisp are Armillaria mellea and Panus stipicus.

A similarly reported phenomena is Fox Fire, which is a gas given off by decomposing wood that is easily ignited and glows sometimes. Phosphine (PH3) ignites spontaneously and might also be produced by decaying organic material but even so would be extinguished quickly by a damp bog, wind and natural expansion. Marsh gas (CH4) apparently does not ignite spontaneously and expands and if blown about, doesn't remain in a small compact mass like certain marsh lights. Swamp gas has often been compared to marsh gas, particularly during the UFO flaps of the 1960s and 1970s certain government officials from Project Bluebook and the Air Force tried to explain away unidentified flying objects as so-called 'swamp gas'.

St. Elmo's Fire is often confused with and/or offered as an explanation for both earth lights and will-o'-the-wisps. However, St. Elmo's fire is not the same phenomenon as has been explained by science. It is an electrical luminescence often observed around masts or other high poles. There are many forms of explained luminescence in the earths atmosphere, for example: aurora borealis, gengenschein, counterglow, astronomical objects, high altitude energy discharges, lightning and the 'glass flash effect' caused by the last rays of the sun becoming bent by the atmosphere as it sets in the west.

Lightning effects can be explained however there are still some lightning related phenomena that we don't understand. These are: Volcanic lightning, ball lightning and sprites and blue jets.

Volcanic lightning is simply lightning that occurs in volcanic eruptions. Sprites and blue jets are discharges that occur above lightning storms, and were only discovered very recently. They have been explained, but because the science is extremely new, it is still slightly vague. While ball lightning is perhaps the most interesting of the three.

William R. Corliss in his marvelous book *Lightning, Auroras, Nocturnal Lights and Related Luminous Phenomena* describes the condition for volcano lights such: "With so much charge-laden dust and steam accompanying volcanic eruptions, conditions exist for all manner of electrical discharges and associated luminous phenomena. Luminous structures may also originate in the powerful shock waves emitted from volcanic craters. In other words, most volcanic lights are probably compatible with the extreme physical conditions generated."

Earthquake lights were included in the synonyms for earth lights, but deserve their own explanation for reasons that shall become apparent. Earthquake lights are lights that are observed during earthquakes near the fault lines involved. What is interesting is they can take on exactly the same characteristics as earth lights, it's just that these are earth lights occurring during earthquakes! These are thought to occur because of tectonic stress upon quartz crystals in the earth's layers which, when rubbed together, create a piezoelectric effect, which we call earthquake lights.

Ball lightning is, as the name suggests, balls of lightning produced in a thunderstorm that are spherical in shape. They usually occur after intense flashes of lightning, and are usually described as 'balls of fire' and not usually lasting more than a few seconds. These balls have very similar properties to earth lights, except ball lightning tends to explode rather violently. One researcher, whom shall remain nameless, even suggested, at one time, that he believed that the occurrences around Joplin, Missouri in conjunction with the Tri-State Spooklight was a form of ball lightning showing up on a regular basis. This is quite absurd because ball lightning is so rare and the Joplin light is seen almost every night from dusk to dawn.

Treasure and money lights are often seen around locations thought to have some kind of buried treasure nearby. When pirates had their loot buried by their crew, those who dug the pit were often killed by the pirates themselves in an attempt to keep the place secret. The lights that are seen at these locations are thought to be the spirits of the unfortunate victims that were employed to bury the treasure.

Orbs, as many of us are aware, are a more recent phenomenon and one that is truly unknown at this time. However, many people have captured these strange orbs on videotape sometimes using Sony night-vision cameras. Others have recorded these strange objects in visible light with ordinary camcorders and sophisticated studio cameras. Usually the orbs are invisible to the naked eye or shoot by so quickly that we cannot see them until the videotape is replayed. They may indeed be some form of energy that either moves too quickly for us to pick us visually and/or is simply invisible except when bombarded with infrared light.

In *Lightning, Auroras, Nocturnal Lights and Related Luminous Phenomena,* Corliss explains what is sometimes called Foo Fighters. "Toward the end of World War II, pilots of all combatants, in all theaters, reported many cases of fireballs pacing their aircraft. The Americans called them Foo Fighters. Foo Fighters have seemingly become part of UFO lore and therefore ignored by scientists, but many of the sightings must have had some physical basis....St. Elmo's Fire may account for some observations but not for those instances where the fireball is well clear of the aircraft surface."

As you, the reader, can plainly see, there are a number of natural and not-so-natural types of phenomena that can mistakenly be interpreted for spooklights. Most of us don't know how to tell the difference though, especially if the occurrence is fairly short-lived and unexpected. However, if you use this work as a guidebook, you can better you chances of seeing something truly paranormal and truly unknown.

Ghost lights seem to be found at or around three distinct geographic instances. Water; lakes, rivers, creeks, oceans, etc., railroad tracks, whether they are still in use or not; and, long rural roads, the lonelier the better. Sometimes two or more of these factor into one single haunting. But one thing is sure, something strange is surely going on at these sites.

Being a veteran researcher and having a very open mind to the subject, I must admit that I became quite spooked at a few of the sites mentioned in this book including the Gurdon light in Arkansas, but mostly at the Joplin Spooklight near Joplin, Missouri. On several times I walked into what I can best discuss as a 'fear zone', something veteran researcher and author John Keel experienced while investigating the famous Mothman case at Point Pleasant, West Virginia. I quote from his outstanding book *The Mothman Prophecies*: "As I passed a certain point on one of the isolated roads I was suddenly engulfed in fear. I stepped on the gas and after I went a few yards my fear vanished as quickly as it came. I continued to drive, eventually returning again to the same spot. And again a wave of unspeakable fear swept over me. I drove quickly away from the place and then stopped, puzzled. Why would this one stretch of road produce this hair-raising effect? I turned around and slowly headed back, trying to note trees, fenceposts, and other landmarks in the dark. Once again when I reached that particular point the hair tingled on the back on my neck and I became genuinely afraid. When I emerged from the other side of this invisible zone I stopped and got out of my car. The air was perfectly still. There wasn't any audible sound...not even a bird call. I was reminded of the hour of quiet that settles inexplicably over the jungle in early morning when suddenly, around 2 a.m., all of the animals, birds, even the insects, become totally silent for about two hours. I walked back to the 'zone of fear' slowly, alert for any rustle of bushes, measuring my own breathing and emotions. I was perfectly calm until I took one step too many and was back in the zone. I almost panicked and ran, but I forced myself to look around and proceed slowly. By now I had figured out that I was probably walking through a beam of ultrasonic waves and really had nothing to be afraid of. After I had gone about fifteen feet I stepped outside the zone and everything was normal again. Now I had to walk through that damned spot again to get back to my car! It was too dark, almost pitch-black, and I was too unfamiliar with the TNT area at the time to attempt to go around the zone. Although I knew it was harmless, I dreaded reentering it. I actually considered remaining there, only yards from my car, until daybreak. But I finally steeled myself and walked once more through that invisible stream, scared out of my wits in transit yet privately pleased with my discovery.

"In daylight I returned to the same spot. The zone of fear was gone. I searched for power transmission lines, telephone microwave towers, and anything that might have radiated energy through the area. There was nothing."

I will describe my passage into a remarkably similar 'zone of fear' in the chapter devoted to Missouri and the Joplin Spooklight. It was an experience I will never forget nor will I forget what happened directly after my passage into the 'zone'.

What actually causes these mysterious lights to suddenly begin appearing is anyone's guess but folklore dictates that ghost lights are commonly seen at locations where some unfortunate person has 'lost his head' in some kind of accident. And, according to folklore, the light that is seen is thought to be the spirit of the deceased who has now come back and is still looking for his head with a lantern! While that probably isn't the case, I believe that there may be some kind of energy that visitors to these mysterious areas are seeing, encountering and photographing. Not all spirits show up as semi-transparent figures resembling a human form; they may simply appear as a ball of light and perhaps that's what lingers at these locations.

Others believe the first theory that the light is actually a residual haunting. In other words, something so tragic that happened it impressed itself into the fabric of time and space and is constantly being replayed over and over again like viewing a videotape. In this case, however, there would be no real intelligence associated with the haunting but simply the energies and anxieties trapped here replaying to the unwary visitor.

I have divided the book into two major sections; alphabetically in the United States by states and by countries. While all states probably have some well-known or little-known phenomena, this author only lists those that has come to his attention in the over 20 years of research into these elusive spooklights. You are invited to contact me to supply additional information on these existing sites or new sites not listed in this book.

So, relax back while I take around the world in search of Spooklights around the world!

Dale Kaczmarek
Holidays 2003-2003

AMERICAN SPOOKLIGHTS

Railroad Tracks Near Crossett, Arkansas where a Spooklight has been Reported for decades

ALABAMA

<u>Cahaba Heights:</u>
(Directions: Take Overton Road exit off Hwy 280. A clump of yellow jonquils marks the spot where the ball of light was first seen.)

A strange ball of light, which has become known as Pegues's Ghost, was seen for many years in a grove of cedars behind the home of Colonel C.C. Pegues, who lived in the house from 1830 to 1860. His house had been used as a jail from 1820 to 1826, and some suggest that the phenomenon may be connected with the spirits who were incarcerated there. The first sighting was in 1862, during the Civil War, when a large, brilliant ball of light was seen hovering a few feet off the ground. The ball chased and teased visitors to the area for years, even after the Pegues' house was torn down.

(Source: National Directory of Haunted Places by Dennis William Hauck)

Molloy:

(Directions: Just south of Hwy 18, near an old well, ten miles west of Vernon)

Another lesser known light has been observed from time to time near the town of Molloy, about ten miles west of Vernon. The light appears just south of Highway 18, near an old well. Some local residents have actually shot at the light, (a more common behavior when confronted by a spook light then you might imagine), but it only became dimmer and more diffused.

Long-time resident, Gardner Lampkin, says the light has been around since he was a youngster and he's seen it many times. Back in those days men shot at the light, "but they never killed it". Lampkin said that before the shots the light would be small and bright, suspended in mid-air. After the shots it would seem to spread out, but it always stayed there.

Vernon:

(Directions: Vernon is located northwestern Alabama along Rt. 17 and 18)

In the town of Vernon, not too terribly far from the much larger town of Florence, stands an old abandoned prison where a strange light has been seen for over a 35-year period. It has been observed regularly between the hours of 5:30 and 11:30 p.m. on practically any clear night. Seen as circular in shape and between eight to twelve feet in diameter with an orange glow, it flies at a slow speed and at an altitude from 300 to 2000 feet. At different times the lights have been seen to pulsate, flicker, hover, blink and then suddenly disappear.

Whatever the object is, it emits a bright orange glow and is usually the brightest object in the sky, second only to the moon. The average sighting lasts from three to six minutes and often three or four of the lights can be observed each night.

Wyatt Cox of Iron City, Tennessee has seen the phenomena on numerous occasions and has photographed it. One 15-second time exposure shows the spook light moving slowly into some trees and was taken at 9:35 p.m. on October 21, 1980. Power lines can be seen in the foreground of the photograph. The light was being investigated at that time by the American Association of Meta Science (AAMS).

ALASKA

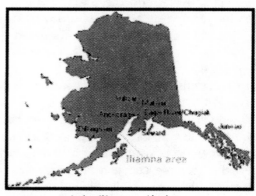

Lake Iliamna, Alaska

Lake Iliamna:
(Directions: Located on the SW tip of Alaska in the Katwai National Preserve about 200 miles SW of Anchorage)

On the Alaska peninsula and along the mountains that encircle Lake Iliamna unusual lights have been observed in the past. Nicknamed "The Iliamna Lights" by local residents, they appear as a brilliant glow. Once observed at Iliamna airfield by personnel, the light was thought to be some forty miles away. One explanation was eliminated by a Mr. Phillip Holdsworth, a former territorial mines commissioner, who stated that the phenomenon wasn't caused by uranium in the mountains.

ARIZONA

Dragoon Mountains:
(Directions: train seen crossing the Alkali Flats in SE Arizona from Dragoon Mountains to the town of Wilcox off I-10 about 50 miles NW of Tombstone)

A ghostly train has been reported running along the plains here. Many have heard the engine's distant whistle or seen its dim yellow headlight from afar. One thing wrong with this story is that there were never any railroad tracks in the area!

(Source: National Directory of Haunted Places by Dennis William Hauck)

ARKANSAS

Crossett:
(Directions: near the Louisiana border in Ashley County on US Hwy 425)
There is a ghost light that is sometimes seen in southeast Arkansas in

Crossett, population 6282, aptly named "The Crossett Light". The story is told about a railroad man who was supposedly decapitated in an accident and eternally searches with a lantern for his lost head. The light appears in a rural area on a gravel road near the Arkansas, Louisiana and Mississippi railroad tracks. There are no houses close to the area and no paved roads. Some lights have been seen high in the trees while others were closer to the tracks.

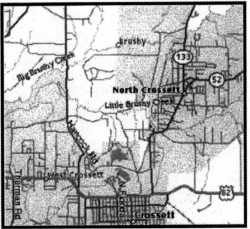
Map of the Crossett Light Area

Dover:
(Directions: located at Rt. 164 and 27 just N of Russellville)

Strange lights appear just a few miles north of Dover, Arkansas. There is a lookout on the side of road looking down into a valley. Below is the Piney Creek. The lights are most often seen on the steep mountainside across the river. There are no houses, no roads or anything else there. Just a forest covered mountainside.

Sometimes there is just one light but at other times more than one. The lights appear to fluctuate in brightness and look like people down there with flashlights going through the woods at night. The lights disappear behind trees, then reappear. People refer to them as the "Dover Lights". One explanation put forth by locals is that the lights are nothing more than light reflecting off the creek. Others aren't so sure.

Gurdon:
(Directions: just of Little Rock, 21 miles south of Arkadelphia on US Hwy 67)

Local residents say it's the lantern carried by the spirit of a murdered railroad man. Others say it's a scientifically explainable phenomenon -- but they can't explain it. Whatever it is, everyone agrees it's there, as residents of southwest and central Arkansas have been seeing the "Gurdon Light" along a four-mile stretch of the Missouri-Pacific Railroad tracks since the early

The railroad tracks where the Gurdon Light has been sighted for many years.

1930s.

A nighttime trek through the dense, swampy woods and past an old cemetery to see the phenomenon reveals a yellowish-white, sometimes bluish, light that appears one to three feet above the tracks about one and a half miles north of Gurdon. The light is thought to be approximately eighteen inches wide, one foot high and shaped like a medicine or rugby ball.

On occasion, it has been seen turning around at one end of the track and later appearing at the other end. The light never gets too close to observers. Photographs of the light have never reproduced well.

The Gurdon Light has a story, a ghostly story, and one that ties into families that still live in the area. It seems a railroad foreman was bludgeoned to death with a spike maul by one of his employees right along the Missouri-Pacific tracks where the light appears (north of Gurdon between state Highway 57 and Interstate 30). The employee had been accused of sabotaging the tracks, trying to wreck the Sunshine Special, but actually causing the wreck of a freight the day before. (No one was killed, according to the December 10, 1931 *Southern Standard*, but a group of hoboes were treated for injuries at Gurdon.)

Alone on the tracks that night with his foreman and angered by the accusation, the story goes, the workman struck him with a shovel. The victim rose and tried to run away, but addled by the blow, he tripped in the sink hole of a rotted stump and fell. The workman finished him off with the spike maul, then walked into Gurdon -- where he was arrested for 'acting suspicious'. After a confession was solicited, a search party found the body. Before collapsing for the final time, the victim had crawled in a trail of blood for nearly a quarter of a mile. The workman was electrocuted for the crime in February of 1932.

Since that time, a lantern has allegedly been seen swinging near the area along the tracks where the foreman was killed, however many prefer the headlight theory. Headlights and taillights have been the single most suggested explanation for many ghost lights. Looking down long stretches of either railroad tracks or rural highways, skeptics believe that the terrain can be confusing in the darkness and what many people think is actually something paranormal is actually only the comings and goings of headlights of distant traffic, sometimes reflected or refracted along the alleged 'haunted' locale.

Dr. Charles Leming, a professor of physics from nearby Arkadelphia College, supervised a study of the Gurdon Light as part of a one-hour credit course called "Physics: Theories - Fact and Fiction." Since the mid-1950s a new wave of college students has descended into the deep night woods, tottered over trestles, toed gingerly over rotting ties and squinted ahead to where a triangle of sky points to the apex of the narrowing railroad tracks where the light has been seen for years.

On a hot evening in June of 1980, a party of 12 professors, students and curious visitors parked their cars at the little-used railroad crossing, smeared their bodies with insect repellant and headed down the tracks that connects Gurdon to Okolona. Dr. Leming led the way followed by Mike Clingan, who headed the investigation. An English major and state chess champion in his third year at the time of the investigation, he had over 140 credits already under his belt. The Gurdon Light had always interested him since he used to make almost nightly visits to the lonely train tracks, sometimes alone!

Local legends abound in the area including an old black cemetery where some guys used to hide by the tombstones to scare people who came to view the light. Reports say they were scared away themselves, but they didn't specify 'by what'. Then there's a hanging tree where unfortunate people were neck-tied while Arkansas was still a territory. Some say if you park underneath that particular tree, your car begins to shake uncontrollably.

It is believed that to view the light properly you must proceed down the tracks for about a mile and a half just beyond the third trestle. In the distance ahead, you could see a yellow, orange or even red light bob around and move from left to right or vice versa. Skeptics will point out however that in direct line of viewing lies the interstate approximately four miles away, a couple of logging roads for four-wheel drive vehicles and Stickey Road; which hasn't been kept up for years. In reality, however, there is a large hill in between, which meant that if the light was caused by passing headlights, it would have to be refracted upland over the hill to be visible on the other side. Some say it could be caused by radiated heat from the tracks bumping into the cooler air above it that would prove to be ideal conditions for refraction or a temperature inversion layer effect. (See Brown Mountain Lights section)

Clingan says he has tested the light for polarization, but found none. "That rules out it being a mirage, because mirage light is half-polarized," he said. Some have theorized the light is caused by swamp gas. But Clingan says he has viewed the light hundreds of times in all types of weather and it always holds shape, which it could not do if caused by swamp gas. Clingan has noticed the light causes a slight deflection in a galvanometer, which measures electric current, indicating the light could be produced by a ball of charged particles held together in a magnetic mirror. Sounds good, but try that on some of the area residents who say they have heard eerie sounds along the tracks as well as viewed the light.

I traveled to Clark County, Arkansas in September of 1984 to conduct my own investigation of the Gurdon Light. I contacted the *Arkansas Gazette,* who published the original article and was accompanied by Lamar James and a photographer, John Cary. Even though there was supposed to be a full moon that evening, it hadn't risen yet and the area was as dark as pitch. You couldn't see more than a few feet ahead of you.

I arrived there with a video and still camera and James provided a set of two-way radios for communication purposes. We continued walking down the tracks for quite a time, listening to unusual sounds; unusual for me I guess, being a city-boy. The reporters tried to ease my fears by offering simply explanations like turtles flopping into the water, even though the noise sounded more like a body falling in to ordinary animal movements. On that night, however, the light was a no-show even though I had seen it the night before - a greenish-blue light arcing from rail to rail in the distance.

After we arrived at the third trestle, we continued for a bit more before the reporters became a bit nervous themselves. We peered down the tracks without any success, so I tried taking some time-lapse photographs with a 35mm camera loaded with high-speed 400 ASA film. The whole time there we saw nothing out of the ordinary, however, on looking at the processed film, I was surprised to see two or three photographs that showed a moving light in an otherwise pitch-black photograph. The shutter was held open manually for over two minutes at one time and nothing else in the pictures could be discerned except this unusual light!

I walked away with a sense of awe and wonderment at the possible cause for this light. A follow-up investigation with topographical and surface maps might shed some more light on this mystery.

Mena:
(Directions: located in NW Arkansas along US Hwy 59/71 and Rt. 8)

This story was posted on the Internet, July 30, 2000:

"I grew up in the little town of Mena, Arkansas and had heard stories of strange occurrences on Rich Mountain all of my life. When I was younger, I used to drive around on that mountain at all times of the day and night and not worry about seeing anything odd or unusual. But one night I saw a glowing light cross the highway in front of my car about seventy-five yards in front of me. It was during summer and I thought that maybe it was someone needing help on the side of the road, but it came down a steep bank and crossed in front of me and then went off the other side of the road in a place that no one could have walked down without killing themselves. I pulled my car to the side of the road and carefully got out and called out to see if it was really someone. When I didn't receive an answer, I got into my car and turned around to leave. A couple of weeks later, I found out a possible explanation for the ghostly light.

"Before the turn of the century, a family of settlers homesteaded a small farm on top of Rich Mountain. At the time, there were very few families on the mountain and it was still a wilderness being settled little by little. During a long, cold Arkansas winter the entire family of a young girl came down sick and she was left to take care of her sick family by cooking and keeping the fire going for heat in their cabin. One evening just before dark, the young girl went out into the woods to gather firewood for the cabin. While she was outside, a pack of wolves chased her up a tall pine tree with nothing but a small kerosene lantern for a light. All night she waited for the wolves to leave. Sometime during the night she died from the freezing cold. The next morning her family discovers her frozen body up in the tree.

"According to the story, she is buried in a small pioneer cemetery not far from where her family's cabin once stood. The ghost light is supposedly this young girl trying to find her sick family so she can take care of them. I have visited this girls grave on the mountain at the little cemetery and to the best of my knowledge, this is a true story."

CALIFORNIA

Borrego Springs:
(Directions: San Diego County, 26 miles north of Octillo on Hwy S2)

Anza-Borrego Desert State Park and the Borrego Springs area of California are notorious for the many legends, ghost stories and unexplained phenomena occurring there over the years. The region of the Sonoran Desert is home to the Vallecito Stage Station, Yaqui Well, in addition to the mysterious "Ghost Lights" of Oriflamme Mountain.

The first account of the "Phantom Lights" of Borrego was reported in 1858 by a Butterfield Stage driver. Since then, soldiers, prospectors and explorers have reported seeing similar lights. The sightings have been reported near Oriflamme Mountain, over Borrego Valley and in other nearby areas. The occurrences are always slightly different, but the general description of the sightings is the same.

In 1892, a prospector by the name of Charles Knowles and two other men were camping near Grapeville Canyon at the entrance to the Narrows, where they reported their sightings of "Fire Balls". Knowles described the lights as balls of fire that rose up approximately 100 feet in the air and then exploded. Knowles compared the fire balls to fireworks. He saw three fire balls rise and cascade upon explosion, before they stopped. About 30 minutes later, the lights started again, but this time they were different. The lights rose into an arch pattern returning to the ground without exploding. The light would then reverse itself and go back to the place where it started.

Scientists have tried to determine a logical explanation for the ghost lights. One scientific explanation suggests that when the wind blows sand against quartz outcroppings, static electricity is created, which could look like bright lights or sparks on a dark night.

Some believe that the lights were signals used by bootleggers during prohibition or U.S. Immigration officials looking for smuggling operations related to the Mexican Border. The only problem with these two explanations is that the sightings have been going on long before modern times and after the time constricted by the events described above.

Another notion is that the fire balls indicate the location of buried treasure. There are legends that support this latter theory. One of the stories tells of a young man who found many gold nuggets in a gully within the Oriflammes. Another man by the name of George Benton found a boulder of rock, weighing a ton, that contained gold. He found the boulder in the

Oriflammes.

Hollister:
(Directions: Pinnacles National Monument between Hollister and King City)

At the Pinnacles National Monument, between Hollister and King City, in the Pinnacles, observers have seen strange lights for quite a number of years. However, in this day and age, they are thought to be earthquake lights because the mountain range straddles the well-known San Andreas Fault, the cause for most of California's numerous earthquakes. A direct cause and effect of piezoelectric discharge, these lights probably have a natural explanation.

Julian:
(Directions: in extreme SW California along Rt. 78 and 79)

Sometimes mountains and mountain ranges can be associated with ghost lights as in the case of the Marfa Lights (to be discussed later) and these multiple lights sometimes seen near the Oriflamme Mountains in San Diego County, along Butterfield Stage Road near Julian, California. They have been allegedly seen since the 1880s and continue to the present day over the mountain range that means "golden flame." The lights were apparently investigated in 1935 by the American Society for Psychical Research and alleged to be "money lights", which supposedly mark gold veins in quartz rock.

In his book *Mysterious Fires and Lights*, author Vincent H. Gaddis suggests some alternate explanations for the Oriflamme Lights. "In bare, dry areas there is quite likely another cause of luminous phenomena on mountains. Scientific studies indicate that the 'Blue Sparks of Khartum' in the Sudan in Africa, as well as similar phenomena at Kano in northern Nigeria, are caused by 'discharging static electricity (which is) generated by the friction of sand particles against one another when they are driven by the wind. (The New York Times, August 1, 1937.)

"In a similar manner, the friction of sand blown against bare desert mountains may at times generate enough static electricity to cause visible discharges at night. This may be the explanation of the 'dancing ghost lights' occasionally seen above the Oriflamme Mountains along the old Butterfield Stage route through the southern California near Julian. (Westways Magazine, April, 1961)."

Many local residents and witnesses to this phenomena don't necessarily agree with that explanation, but of course, they sometimes don't wish to have their local legends bashed.

<u>Santa Susana:</u>
(Directions: on Hwy 118 in western Ventura County)
This ghost town was a Pentecostal Christian commune from 1914 to 1921. The faithful held twenty-four prayer vigils in a brick tower overlooking the community. Now the area is haunted by a floating, square-shaped white light, which moves slowly through the trees and deserted buildings. Some have suggested that it is the spirit of Dr. Finis Yoakum, founder of the commune.
(Source: National Directory of Haunted Places by Dennis William Hauck)

COLORADO

<u>Westcliffe:</u>
(Directions: at the junction of Hwy 69 and Hwy 96 in Custer County is south-central Colorado; cemetery is in Silver Cliff, near Rosita in the foothills of Wet Mountain)
Jim Little has seen 'em -- the mysterious lights that flit through the Silver Cliff Cemetery on the darkest of nights. They're called ghost lights and Little, a rational man by all appearances, says they're real.
"Almost anybody who's an old-timer around here has seen them," says Little, editor/publisher of the *Wet Mountain Tribune*, a weekly newspaper that's been in existence since 1883. "It's just one of those quirky things, a phenomenon that's never been explained. One of life's mysteries."
The ghost lights are silver-dollar sized, round and whitish. They usually appear three or four at a time, dancing and floating among headstones in the main Silver Cliff Cemetery south of town. Founded in 1878, this Catholic cemetery also contains an old Spanish section and is marked by an old rotted wood sign, at last report. They're ephemeral and tend to disappear just when you're trying to get a closer look. The lights were written about in the August 1969 issue of *National Geographic* and are now considered part tourist attraction, part folklore of the Wet Mountain Valley.
The ghost lights are usually best seen during new-moon nights. They're never been captured in photographs and they've never been glimpsed in the Catholic cemetery, which is about a mile away from the main cemetery.
Possible theories to the lights' origin are reflections of the town lights of Silver Cliff and Westcliffe or that they are phosphorus, perhaps from deteriorated tombstones to methane gas. Geologists and ghost-debunkers have failed to prove any of those theories as fact, though.

So does that mean they're ghosts? "I don't know," Little says with a smile, "but that's the widest-held theory."

Sometimes the lights have appeared bluish in color and many local residents indicate that the area has been active since the Spring of 1956, even though the lights were first observed in 1880 when Silver Cliff was at its boomtown height, with a population of five thousand. They have been observed as large as basketballs and appear to pulsate at times.

Bill Kleine, who once ran a local campground, says he's seen the lights plenty of times. Best times are overcast evenings with no moon. Dim, round spots of blue-white light glowed ethereally among the graves when Kleine visited the cemetery with Edward Linehan and the *National Geographic* crew in 1969. For 15 minutes, they walked about the place, pursuing one will-o'-the-wisp, then another. The crew surmised that the nearby towns were just too far away to reflect the lights onto the old tombstones but they assumed anything was possible.

"Only trouble is," said Bill, "my wife and I have both seen these lights when the fog was so thick you couldn't see the towns at all."

Linehan cited the theory of anthropologist and folklorist Dale Ferguson that the Cheyenne and other Plains Indians buried their dead on 'hilltops sacred to the spirits.' A number of Indian legends speak of 'dancing blue spirits' on such sites.

Old timers in the Silver Cliff area have quite another explanation; they will tell you that the lights are the helmet lamps of long-dead miners still searching for silver on the hilltops.

The lights continued to be seen over the years, and in 1967 a story about them appeared in *The New York Times*.

"No doubt someone, someday, will prove there's nothing at all supernatural in the luminous manifestations at Silver Cliff's cemetery," Linehan concludes. "And I will feel a tinge of disappointment."

Theories abound from reflections from the stars, phosphorescent ore, hoaxers with luminous paint, to reflections of the mercury vapor of the Westcliffe street lights (but during a power failure the lights remained undimmed, and there were no mercury vapor streetlights in 1880).

DELAWARE

Cape Henlopen State Park:
(Directions: Cape Henlopen is at the entrance to Delaware Bay. The park

is 17 miles NE of Georgetown at the end of Hwy 404)

A cylindrical shaft of rough stone rises out of the mist here and shines a flickering beacon at ships approaching the coast. Locals have dubbed it a Corpse Light; some a Bad Weather Witch, because even though it looks like a legitimate lighthouse, it isn't. It has caused numerous deaths. The first dating back to December 25, 1655 when the *Devonshireman* crashed on the rocks killing almost two hundred people.

FLORIDA

<u>Cedar Key:</u>
(Directions: overlooking the Gulf of Mexico along Rt. 24)

In 1954, R.B. Davis of Cedar Key, Florida, his brother Tilden Davis, of Chiefland, and Oliver Holmes, a retired railroader, set off from a camp on the Hall River for Cedar Key. Strong winds sprung up and soon caused the boat to capsize. In the darkness, the three men clung desperately to the boat.

Shortly thereafter, the they noticed a red light in the distance. It moved back and forth as if to attract their attention. Breaking loose a seat from the boat to use as a paddle, the three took turns rowing toward the light. The light continued to move in front of them and they followed. Shortly before dawn, the trio hit land. They never did determine the origin of the light or what became of it!

<u>Gainesville:</u>
(Directions: near Gainesville on Williston Road)

Located somewhere near Gainesville and perhaps down old Williston Road out beyond the city limits, a strange light was first reported here in the late '50s or early '60s.

Back before the encroachment of urban sprawl and its artificial lights, the county roads in central Florida could get very dark on moonless nights. It was on one such night that a man was driving home rather late. It was warm, and he had his driver-side window down, his left arm resting along the edge as he drove. After a few miles, he saw a single light coming toward him, close to the dividing line in the middle of the road. As dark as it was, he couldn't actually see the vehicle, but he assumed it was a motorcycle. It wasn't. It was actually a semi-truck whose driver was either drunk or asleep at the wheel -- its left headlight was burned out, so all the man saw was the right headlight as the truck barreled down the middle of the road and plowed into him. The man was killed instantly. The arm that he'd had resting in the window was severed and flung into the woods, and one of the headlights was knocked clear of the wreckage. Later, officials at the scene of the crash searched and searched for the arm and the headlight, but neither was ever recovered.

That's the background. Now, if you drive out to that lonely stretch of road on moonless nights and park your car over on the shoulder and wait, eventually you'll see a light. One such report came from a couple who decided to see if the stories were indeed true. They went out there as a prank and saw a light way off in the distance, and gradually it got closer and closer until it seemed to literally touch their windshield and vanish.

They say that it's the accident victim out with the headlight that the police never found still searching for his missing arm!

Jacksonville:
(Directions: located in extreme NE Florida at the junction of I-10 and I-95 in St. John's County Greenbrier or Light Road runs east off Hwy 13 about 7 miles S of the Duval County Line)

This mysterious ball of concentrated light, called the "Greenbriar Light," seems to be attracted to moving objects. Cars moving slowly down the road in either direction bring out the light, which follows between 25 to 300 feet behind. Occasionally the light moves over the cars, but it never passes them. In 1987, the St. John's County Sheriff's Department asked several scientists to investigate the phenomenon, but no definite conclusion as to the source of the light could be reached. According to local legend, the light is the headlight of a phantom motorcycle. A young man was supposedly pushing he new motorcycle to maximum speed on the road when he lost control and hit the support cable of a telephone pole. His decapitated body was found the next day.

(Source: National Directory of Haunted Places by Dennis William Hauck)

Oviedo:
(Directions: State Rd. 13 in Seminole County)

Located in Seminole County, multiple lights have been for a number of years along State Road 13.

(Source: Atlas of the Mysterious in North America by Rosemary Ellen Guiley)

GEORGIA

Cogdell:
(Directions: south Georgia along Rt. 122 and 187)

The small town of Cogdell was famous in south Georgia and north Florida for its spook light. It was visible on a dead end road that paralleled the old train track. As the legend goes, a conductor was killed in a train accident and was decapitated. The light was supposedly from his lantern as he searched for his head. (Very similar stories are told elsewhere across the country.)

The owner of a nearby motel in the county related that she remembered travelers coming to Clinch County specifically to attempt to see the light in the early 1960s.

Most of the reports were that the light would follow vehicles for miles, then disappear abruptly. Cynics said that it was swamp gas or hunters with flashlight helmets. One report from a local stated that he remembered as a child that his uncle and aunt took him to look for the light. They parked in the center of the road and would sit absolutely quiet in order to see it.

The most recent first-hand report came from a person who encountered the phenomena without ever having heard of it. She had just moved to the area from up north, and to say the least was shaken by the event, and even more concerned when the locals told her not to worry, "that was just the Cogdell Spooklight."

Screven:
(Directions: Seaboard Coast Line between Screven and Jesup, on US Hwy 82 and Rt. 169)

Their car straddled a railroad track at a secluded dirt road crossing just outside of town as they watched and waited. It was between ten and midnight on a Saturday, and the night was pitch black. The crammed carload of young men and women, like others before them, had come to see proof of the 'ghost light' in this south Georgia town.

"That's it. That's the ghost light," whispered the driver of the car. No one disputed his word. A local railroad employee, the young man was familiar with every signal light along the track.

They watched for a while, hoping or dreading....that the strange glow would never venture closer. It never did. But on past nights, dating as far back as the Civil War, the eerie light has been seen to loom much closer.

Jim Henry Bennett, a Screven native, claims to have witnessed the light, which is usually sighted late at night, often after a rain, when a train has recently passed near Milligan's Crossing. Witnesses to the Screven ghost light all describe its presence with similar words... "a glowing clear-white ball that floats and swings side to side along the tracks, its light often flashing bright, then dimming."

One alleged tale has it that the bobbing light is a swinging lantern carried by the ghost of a railroad flagman killed years in a train accident. The ghost wanders along the tracks of the Seaboard Coast Line between Screven and Jesup, searching for his head, which was allegedly severed in the accident.

Another story says the light is the ghost of one of many railroad workers whose bodies were buried alongside the tracks during the railroad's construction shortly after the Civil War.

Andy Lastinger, the town's fire chief, said many residents laugh off the legends, but no one has been able to fully explain what causes the light to appear. "We've had scientists come down here to look at it, but nothing ever came out of it," Lastinger said.

One theory is that the glow is a reflection from low-hanging gases floating near the tracks from a nearby marsh. Another explanation is that the light is being seen miles away from the city of Jesup.

"I don't think anyone will ever really know what it is," Lastinger said. "There's definitely something there - and we've just come to live with it."

Surrency:
(Directions: about 125 miles from Macon, near Jesup on Hwy 82)
The Surrency Spook Light is a classic example of the ghost light phenomena in the best tradition of the more famous ones, such as the Marfa Lights and the Brown Mountain Lights. The site of the Surrency Light is centralized along a stretch of the Macon/Brunswick railway that runs through Surrency, Georgia.

A Mr. James Joyner, of nearby Baxley, has witnessed the light several times. He described how he was standing on the train track at night when the light appeared several hundred yards in front of him, hovering over the railway. Mr. Joyner's description of the light was "a very bright, golden-yellow light, about the size and shape of a grapefruit." When he tried to approach the light, it began to move toward him until it finally blinked out, only to reappear behind him!

The Surrency Light has been an observable phenomena since the turn of the century. Explanations for the light vary from the local belief that it is somehow connected to the famous Surrency ghost that haunted the hotel/home of A.P. Surrency (for whom the town is named) to a mysterious geological formation underneath the ground in Surrency, as theorized by Cornell University professor Larry Brown.

Allen Powell Surrency first settled the area in the early 1850s when the area was mostly forests and swamps and unclaimed. Mr. Surrency opened a sawmill in what would later become the town of Surrency. The Surrency's opened their home as a rooming house to accommodate travelers, some stayed there, while others would spend the night in the old Camping Ground near Surrency and swap hair-raising stories. The Surrency ghost appeared at the A.P. Surrency's house in 1872, and the exciting and unexplained happenings gave the campers at the Camp Ground something to talk about for years.

A.P. Surrency sent the following news article to the Savannah Morning News and it was published October 23, 1872.

Please allow me a small place in your paper to publish a strange freak of nature. On Thursday last, I returned from Station Number 8 ½ (Hazelhurst) to my residence at Station Number 6, Macon and Brunswick Railroad where I have lived for twenty years unmolested. On my arrival at home about 7 o'clock p.m. I found my family and some of my neighbors, among them Reverend Benjamin Blitch, Colonel D.W. Roberts, my brother and several others whom I consider men of truth, very much excited.

In a few minutes after my arrival at home I saw the glass tumblers begin to slide off the slab and the crockery to fall upon the floor and break. The books began to tumble from their shelves to the floor, while brick bats, billets of wood, smoothing irons, biscuits, potatoes, tin pans, water buckets, pitchers, etc.; began to fall in different parts of my house. Nearly all my crockery and glasses have been broken. There have been many other strange occurrences about my house. These facts can be established by 75 to 100 witnesses. Yours in haste, A.P. Surrency."

Hundreds of personal accounts from diaries, as well as books and magazines, have described tables flying through the air, mirrors exploding in hallways, clocks running wild after witnesses heard a mysterious buzzing noise, hot bricks falling from the sky, lights flickering in the dark, and unexplained voices screaming, crying or laughing in and around the Surrency house.

There were numerous other articles published in newspapers across the State of Georgia by reporters who braved the night at the Surrency home and by family members. Surrency became *the* place to visit because of the ghost. The Surrency house was destroyed by fire in 1925 and the Surrency family moved to another home, however, the ghost did not follow them.

The Surrency bright spot was found in a regional seismic survey in 1985, which was searching for the suture, or join, between the ancient North American and African continents. The survey discovered an usually strong reflection of sound waves from a depth of about nine miles. This "bright spot", scientists speculate, is a small bowl-shaped reflector facing upwards. It seems likely the Surrency Bright Spot is some unusually dense material that was caught up in the process of collision between Africa and North America millions of years ago.

"It's big, and we've never seen anything like it before," says Dr. Larry Brown, an associate professor of geological sciences at Cornell University, who was part of a scientific team that discovered the formation.

Dr. Brown is a director of the Cornell University-based Consortium for Continental Reflective Profiling (COCORP), which is developing a detailed picture of the Earth's mantle.

"It might have something to do with the Surrency's ghost," says Mayor Stanford Tillman. "If this town is know for anything, it's for the ghost that supposedly haunted the old Surrency house owned by the family for whom the town is named during the 1870s and 1880s."

HAWAII

Waimea:
(Directions: Hawaii island)
On the big island of Hawaii situated on the old Parker Ranch strange lights were said to appear close to midnight on the first two to three nights of the New Moon. Nicknamed "The Waimea Lights", they were seen drifting over the plains and vanishing near the Mauna Kea Volcano. Some witnesses have heard music drifting out from the cores of the glowing balls.

ILLINOIS

Greenwood Cemetery:
(Directions: Decatur is located in central Illinois on US Hwy 51 near I-72)
Greenwood Cemetery was founded in 1857 on forty acres of land. Today, however, there are well over 100 acres of beautiful sloping hills, tall trees and wide expanses of grassland.

The hills where the Ghost Lights of Greenwood Cemetery are still seen

The ghost lights that plague this cemetery are always seen on the far south side of the graveyard. Witnesses claim the lights bob and move among the gravestones displaying some form of intelligent control. It has been suggested as reflections of cars passing the area, but according to those who have seen them, they surely aren't car lights!

In the late 1800s, the Sangamon River flooded this area of the cemetery knocking over tombstones and unearthing a number of coffins. Many of which floated with the flooding waters. After the flood it was almost impossible to tell who was who, so many of them were buried on the high hill where the lights are now seen in unmarked graves. The legend is that the lights are those unfortunate spirits who are still not at rest due to being disinterred and buried again.

Joliet:
(Directions: south of Chicago at the junction of I-80 and US Hwy 52)
During a peculiar thunderstorm on March 21, 1916, blue fireballs were seen. Over 20 windows were broken. The windows later turned a strange burned color. Perhaps the effect of ball lightning??

Midlothian:
(Directions: Midlothian Turnpike, just east of Ridgeland Avenue and across from Rubio Woods Forest Preserve)
The small and abandoned Bachelor's Grove Cemetery, located in unincorporated Midlothian/Oak Forest is located on the Midlothian Turnpike just east of Ridgeland Avenue, across from Rubio Woods Forest Preserve. This location is the most haunted site that I've ever come across (see *Windy City Ghosts*). It also has been the scene of a number of ghost light-type phenomena over the years.

Through the mid-1970s, reports began to circulate of mysterious blue balls of light that would apparently drift and float through the cemetery and seemed to display some form of intelligent control. In other words, when chased, they would 'wink out' and then reappear behind the pursuer! A Joliet man named Jack Hermanski chased the ghost light on two occasions. He said the light blinked at ten to twenty second intervals and claimed that the light grew as large as a basketball and changed positions very rapidly.

Denise Travers said that she encountered the light in December of 1971. She related that she had put her hand through the ghost light! She claimed to have felt no heat, nothing at all.

There are those who offered that the lights were nothing more then the gases given off by decomposing bodies but since the last official burial at Bachelor's Grove Cemetery was in 1965, I don't believe that to be the case. Besides that doesn't explain those close encounters.

Another more recent light that has been sighted at the cemetery appears along the dirt trail leading into the cemetery. Numerous reports have been circulated about late night visitors encountering what they have described as a red, sky-rocket zooming up and down the trail and repeating itself in quick succession. The light has been described as brilliant red and makes absolutely no noise whatsoever when it's observed. These lights are still occasionally being spotted from time to time.

Milford:
(Directions: Kankakee County, along Rt. 1 S of Watseka)

It was nearly midnight. Four college students and a professor stood silent at the edge of a country road near Milford. They peered into a grove surrounded by dark fields for a glimpse of a lantern carried by someone or something unseen. They were not on a ghost hunt. Rather, this June evening they were playing the role of folklorists, investigating a local legend. Near a grove of trees in farmland between Crescent City and Milford, a kerosene lantern appears on hot summer nights, the tale goes.

According to one version, the lantern was carried before the turn of the century by a farmer searching in a blizzard for his wandering cows. The farmer never returned but for decades his lantern has been seen glowing in the night. The tale possibly was first told before 1900, because references to it were made years ago by elderly people now deceased, said a woman living near the site of the lantern's alleged appearances. The woman also recounted another version of the tale which says the lantern was carried by a farmer's wife looking for her husband who never returned because he was eaten by his pigs. (The Watseka spook light is located just slightly northeast of this location which makes me wonder if it's the same light, just seen from a different angle with different stories and explanations for it's origin.)

Papineau:

(Directions: Kankakee County, along Rt. 1 S of Kankakee)

The young boy stood motionless in the chilling breath of an autumn dusk, transfixed by the dim and distant figures that labored in the lantern's glow.

"You know, Jacob, you're in as much trouble as I am! If you don't keep quiet - you'll go to jail!" the woman warned her companions.

Afraid to move - afraid even to breath, the boy watched the yellow light swing gently from the cottonwood limb. The woman, and the one called Jacob, continued to dig as the lantern, nudged by an evening breeze, swept its yellow low light back and forth across the fearsome scene.

In time, the digging stopped. The pair turned to the buckboard, it's horse tethered to the tree, then struggled to unload their hidden cargo. They dropped their limp burden into the hole, then quickly covered it with earth. In minutes, it was done.

The lantern, still swinging slowly from the limb, was taken down and quenched. In the darkness, nine-year-old Calix Reno heard the leather lines of the buckboard snap and the horse begin to move. The clatter of its wooden floorboards grew fainter in the distance. And then there was silence.

The legend of Jacob's Lantern began on this desolate Iroquois County night, in the year of 1859. It continues today, with the occasional autumn sighting of a strange light moving from the site of an old roadhouse to the old barn on the hill. If it's true, as some believe, that the souls of the damned can never rest, then the murderers of a Danville cattle drover will replay this grisly night forevermore.

Lee Ponton, who now lives on the property where this murder took place, has seen the eerie lantern twelve times. The last time in November of 1987. But he remembers sightings as a child. On the day following the strange movements of the yellow lantern light out the family's north kitchen window, his father would put Holy Water on the palms of his hands before venturing up to the old corral site. And his mother would sprinkle Holy Water about the house, when night noises outside the windows accompanied the sightings.

If you travel east of Papineau, then take the road to Aroma north across Beaver Creek some crisp autumn night and chance to see a yellow lantern light weaving up the hill to your right, lock the doors and drive more quickly for a ghost may be about.

Watseka:

(Directions: eastern Illinois, 50 miles south of Chicago on Hwy 1, light seen on 1200N between 1980E and 1500E)

Watseka, Illinois, located about 70 miles south of the Chicago Loop is the scene of another (although possibly the same light that is seen from Milford) spook light. Seen along a stretch of 1500N, it is known to locals as "Red Lantern Road" in honor of the spectral red light that is said to travel down the road, carried by the ghost of an old woman who lived on the farm behind the curtain of trees south of the road. She's said to be searching for her husband who went out one winter night and never came back.

I visited this site, along with members of the *Ghost Research Society* and Jo McCord from the *Kankakee Journal* in June of 1991 to observe this light. With the help of locals we were able to narrow the location where the light is most often seen. It appears along a narrow strip of road just west of 1500E between a one-lane bridge and a stone mailbox. Nice landmarks, huh? However, these were easy to find once we found the correct road.

We began our excursion on "Red Lantern Road" at 1500E, about three miles west of Happy Hollow intersection at 4 p.m. Equipped with two-way radios, sound and video recording equipment, a one-million candle-power spotlight and compasses, we used a car's odometer and found that the lights people have been seeing down the road can actually be seen over a mile away even though there were some hills in between.

Interviews with local residents found few positive responses when asked if they had seen the light. I attribute that to the fact that the area is sometimes used as a 'party area' by local teenagers and several stop signs and other traffic signs showed indications of bullet holes! So, I assumed, even if local residents had seen something either natural or supernatural, they probably wouldn't have attested to the fact, just to keep the population around the area at night down to zero.

Those that had an encounter described the light as round and some attribute various colors to it. It is unlikely swamp gas because that source would produce a vertical vapor rather than a round light. There could be a legitimate phenomena here, but I would speculate that the majority of the sightings are nothing more than car headlights in the distance that appear to be much closer than they truly are.

Willow Springs:
(Directions: Maple Lake is on 95th Street between LaGrange Road and Willow Springs Road)

The area along Archer Avenue in south suburban Willow Springs, Illinois has been the scene of a yellow ball of light about the size of a basketball that disappears as you approach it. It has most often been seen as you travel north-northeasterly on Archer Avenue towards Willow Springs and Fairmont Hills Cemetery. Somewhere just before you exit the forest preserve and enter the actual town, the light inexplicably disappears! The light is not animal eyes illuminated by your headlights or warning signs in the distance lit up by high-beams. The light has since disappeared altogether and is not seen along Archer Avenue.

Maple Lake

However, at Maple Lake, 95th Street and Wolf Road, a true ghost light is still being perceived on occasion across the lake as visitors sit and park at the Maple Lake Overlook. This ghost light has been described as a brilliant red, almost laser-beam in intensity, and shines on the far shore of the lake, approximately 1000 feet at it's closer approach.

The customary explanations such as car headlights and taillights simply don't work here for two reasons --- first of all, after dark there is absolutely no way for an automobile to drive on the other side of the lake as the picnic areas are locked and chained up by the forest rangers. Secondly, the next east/west thru street is 107th Street and it is situated on the other side of a high, intervening ridge, called the Sag Ridge. There is no way you can see car headlights or taillights through solid earth!

The light has been reported since the 1950s with it's peak in the late 1970s and early 1980s. Although I've never seen it myself, the best viewing time has always been after 10:30 p.m., if you can dodge the Forest Rangers who will ask you to leave, if not ticket you, for illegal parking after dusk. The light's major shortcoming is irregularity as it does not appear with the frequency of other more well-known ghost lights.

Average sightings last from a few seconds to about a minute or two with long periods of inactivity. Some claim that the light is the spirit of a headless Indian chief still wandering the area as there were many Indian villages dotted up and down Archer Avenue, including St. James Sag Church and Cemetery, which is situated on ancient Indian burial grounds.

While widening and paving Archer over a pre-existing Indian trail workers accidentally unearthed skeletal remains most likely of previously buried Indians. Perhaps this is what is being observed from across the lake from time to time?

There were rumors that there used to be a railroad on the far side of the lake and some old road houses. I could not verify such reports but, if true, it would certainly add another ingredient in the making of ghost light, i.e. water and railroad tracks.

I hope in the near future to conduct an sanctioned overnight investigation at Maple Lake and perhaps see first-hand this mysterious and elusive light.

INDIANA

Dixon's Lanterns:
(Directions: Tunnelton is located in south central Indiana, SE of Bedford and near The Devil's Backbone)

This light is named after a railroad watchman named "Dixon" who died in a train tunnel just east of Tunnelton in 1906 while inspecting the bricks the railroad companies lined their tunnels with at the time. He was allegedly murdered in the tunnel with a single blow to the head with a pick. Dixon was buried in nearby Procter Cemetery, next to Dixon Chapel, about three miles north of Fort Ritner, just over the Jackson County Line.

Within a few years, numerous people began seeing mysterious lights floating in the dark tunnel and it's definitely not another light from the other end or an approaching train as the tunnel curves slightly so that the opposite entrance cannot be seen. The lights that are seen are multiple lights apparently swinging from side to side.

Francisville:
Directions: I-294 south from Chicago, I-65 south to Rt. 30 east, 421 south to Francisville)

A red or yellow, sometimes white, ball of light haunts a rural road just outside of Francisville, Indiana. Often called "The Moody Light" in respect to a local legend concerning a farmer Moody who either was killed by chasing the killers of his daughter or by continuing to search for his daughter's body with a lantern on the night of her disappearance. You can take your pick, as there's nothing in the past history vaguely resembling this story.

The light is again seen at a distance and never close up. There's a long rural road stretching ahead of the viewer for a couple of miles. Locals say there's a tree or tree stump that marks the sight where the disaster happened long ago. If you wait silently in your car and face it down the long rural road and flash your lights on and off three times in succession, the light will suddenly appear and move closer to you.

I have investigated this location twice in the past. The last time with researchers Stan Suho of the *Ghost Research Society* and Gary Hart. By using county maps and two separate sets of directions for finding the exact spot, we were able to finally pinpoint the correct viewing location. It was just a matter of waiting until dark and it wasn't long before we were seeing some lights at the end of the road that appeared to be getting closer before mysteriously vanishing instantly with apparently no where for them to disappear to!

After we viewed a few more of these sightings, with high-powered binoculars and spotting scopes, it soon became apparent that these were definitely car headlights approaching on a parallel road before turning off onto a road that was perpendicular and slightly below our visible horizon. The lights quite nicely diffused into two distinct automobile headlights. We had solved the mystery, much to the chagrin of some area locals who were curious as to what all the equipment was and what we were doing. Again, locals often don't enjoy having their local legends squashed by either skeptics, debunkers or serious researchers looking for logical and explainable answers.

Indianapolis:
(Directions: located in Indianapolis on West Merrill Street near the White River)
An old abandoned house from the late 19th Century was considered to be the best viewing spot for ghostly lights for quite a number of years. It seems on cold winter nights, strange mists and glowing orbs were often observed rising from the White River, drifting up the bank, and through the windows of the abandoned house. Witnesses said that often immediately after the strange orbs entered the empty building, loud low laughter and a kind of song-like moaning would be heard from deep within the building.

Leesburg Lights:
(Directions: located on a rural road between Leesburg and North Webster)
An inexplicable orb of light is sometimes encountered on a very rural road midway between Leesburg and North Webster and sandwiched between South Bend and Fort Wayne. Reports claim the light bobs up and down but may occasionally chase or follow onlookers as they attempt to leave the area.

IOWA

St. Mary's:
(Directions: half-mile south of St. Mary's in Warren County)

A single incandescent light has been seen on a nearby farm close, to the town of St. Mary's. Since 1874, a glowing light has been seen around the perimeter of a 160-acre tract of the Storz farm. The light was said to be 15 or 20 inches in diameter, bright red in the center, and shading to orange at the edge. It would flash bright, intermittent signals then dim. Although it usually traveled in the same horizontal plane close to the ground, some observers said they saw it shoot straight up into the sky. Several young people tried to catch the light at various times, but none were successful.

Some say the light to be the spirit of a Mrs. Wallace who had supposedly burned to death in a house that once stood on the Storz land. However, this story has yet to be authenticated.

The light was particularly active in the 1930s. The owner of a nearby general store, a Mr. C.A. McNair, saw the light while driving home late one evening. He allegedly observed the light simply hanging on the south edge of the Storz farm.

A local farmer, Orval Berning, had also seen the light numerous times throughout his lifetime. On a cold winter early morning, around 1:30 a.m., he was walking home from a card game with some friends. He noticed a strange glow floating along just inside the fence line of the farm. He also claimed that the light often could be seen from the windows of his home, which was almost a mile away from the Storz farm. Most agree that the light remained on the farm for unknown reasons.

However, there is one story that contradicts the above. Nobel Nixon was riding his horse home one evening when the steed became quite agitated and bolted. There, in the middle of the road, was the ghost light. The horse gave him the ride of his life right up to his doorstep.

The light lasted right into the 1940s and was seen as late as 1947 by Roy Whitehead of Indianapolis. While observing the light one evening, he was shocked to hear a disembodied voice apparently emanating from the orb!

KANSAS

Elkhart:
(Directions: located in extreme SW Kansas along Rt. 27 just N of US Hwy

56)

The *Dodge City Daily Globe* reported in November of 1922 that there was a spook light of some kind reported on a certain rural schoolhouse yard, a few miles from Elkhart. The light was described as "a reflection of a big full moon, about the size of a windmill wheel, of a dull red color, shining brightly on a dark night." It was dubbed the "Moonshine Mystery" by local residents.

One report went on to say that one evening a group of boys jumped on their horses in an attempt to chase the light. The orb always seemed to stay about a quarter of a mile ahead of their galloping steeds. When they stopped and decided to give up the chase, the light also stopped and when they decided to retrace their steps back home, the light began to chase them in the opposite direction. They chased it for over an hour.

The Holmes Ghost Light:
(Directions: Brewster, west of Colby on US Hwy 24 in Thomas County)

This light is alleged to be the spirit of one Gilbert Holmes who was dragged to his death by his mules. He was buried in nearby Fairview Cemetery on County Road BB. It wasn't long as his death that two local men were riding through the area and they were confronted by a mysterious light. The light appeared to emanate from the interior of the old Holmes house, now abandoned on the prairie.

The light penetrated the wall of the house and moved outside in the form of a ray-like beacon. The beacon led them along a path directly towards Fairview Cemetery, where it entered the graveyard, hovered over a grave and then vanished from sight! The name on the marker where the curious light had disappeared was Gilbert Holmes!

In either 1907 or 1908, Gilbert Holmes' widow had the body of her husband removed from the cemetery and buried in eastern Kansas. Since that time not a single report of the ghost light has been observed by any local residents. Perhaps Holmes just wished to be closer to his widowed wife.

Mystic Cow Lights:
(Directions: western Kansas near the town of Wallace on US Hwy 40)

In March of 1931, western Kansas was the victim of a severe blizzard and ice storm so bad that several hundred head of cattle were found dead all over the plains. Of course, the task of disposing of these cows was tremendous and many lay on the prairies for days before they could be gathered up and removed.

Allegedly, all the following summer, spook lights were seen in the area. Sometimes the lights were seen to run along the ground, moving just above the earth in a group, like a herd of cattle. Other times the luminous orbs seemed to rise up into the air sharply.

One theory was that the gases from the decomposing bodies was producing these strange glows in the area at night. The lights were only seen on quiet, calm evenings without even the hint of a breeze in the air. They apparently stopped soon after all the cattle were buried and taken away.

KENTUCKY

Haldeman:
(Directions: about 42 miles E of Lexington off I-64 on Rt. 32)

In rural Haldeman, just outside of Morehead, a mysterious light was first seen in the 1950s by some folks visiting from neighboring Ohio. Their great grandmother lived on top of a hill and would often see a light moving between two mountains in the distance. Sometimes it would move from one mountain top to another along the dirt roads prevalent in the area. The main road was right below the great grandmother's house.

According to the report, the light had been there since her mother was a little girl and once a group of men tried to locate the source of the light, however, when they arrived at the location where it had always been observed in the past, they saw nothing (no light).

The legend is that there is some kind of treasure buried around the site and the owner of the booty is trying to find it or lead someone to it by lighting up the area with what looks like a swinging lantern traveling just above the tree tops.

Mt. Sterling:
(Directions: located between Jeffersonville and Means, S of Mt. Sterling on Hwy 460)

At or about the turn of the last century, mysterious lights were seen on the slopes of the Sand Mountains. First hand accounts often claim that the lights would appear along the roads and paths of the mountain, sometimes acting as if they had an intelligence and following travelers as they passed nearby. One man claimed that a "ghost light" often appeared along a certain stretch of road, hovered in the air and then vanished.

Today, the area near the mountain is much more populated than in years past and few still speak of the "ghost lights". Some have suggested that natural gas wells may have caused the phenomena but no one really knows for sure.

LOUISIANA

<u>Gonzales:</u>
(Directions: gravel road between Gonzales and Galvez in east Ascension Parish)

Beginning in April 1951, newspaper reports told of a bright light seen along a stretch of gravel road between Gonzales and Galvez, Louisiana. The sheriff, at the time, Hickley Waguespack, of East Ascension Parish, related that it had a "yellowish cast" but was not bright enough to actually create a beam. Many assumed that Waguespack was attempting to rule the headlight theory brought forth but a number of people at the time.

It has since been declared inactive and hasn't been seen since the early 1950s.

MARYLAND

The Road in Hebron, Maryland where the Light was reported

<u>Hebron:</u>
(Directions: Hwy 347 in Wicomico County in eastern Maryland, six miles NW of Salisbury off US Hwy 50; light was seen on current Church Street)

The Maryland State Troopers had their hands full just before midnight on the clear but steamy night of July 16, 1952. Trooper Robert W. Burkhardt and a sergeant were on routine patrol just a mile west of Hebron, Maryland and had just turned onto Church Street, Extended, a mile-long stretch of road line by trees on both sides. Off in the distance, a circular yellow ball of light was observed slightly above the road and moving toward the car.

"It's either an old car with one dim light or a wagon lantern that should be red," the sergeant was quoted as saying in *Mysterious Fire and Lights* by

Vincent Gaddis.

Whatever it was began to rapidly close on the vehicle, moving directly in the middle of the road. At the last possible moment, to avoid a collision, the trooper swerved off the road unto the shoulder and skidded to a rather abrupt stop. According to the two troopers, the light suddenly stopped and hovered in the glare of their headlights approximately twenty feet away. As they restarted the car and began to approach the object, it receded. And as they gained speed toward the light, the object matched the squad's speed and kept the same distance. As the car reached a speed of forty miles per hour, the light inexplicably vanished!

Not wanting to risk ridicule, Burkhardt returned the following night with five other patrolmen and found the light was already there on Church Street waiting for them. They all exited their vehicles and attempted to surround the light, which abruptly winked out and then reappeared in a nearby field!

Several days afterwards, additional officers, including Edward H. Bracey, pursued the object for over a half-mile before the globe veered off the road at fifty miles per hour into a field.

"It was just like a neon tube when you turn it out," Burkhardt said. "It faded slowly into a reddish glow which finally went out."

Lieutenant C.C. Serman, commander of the State Police Barracks in nearby Salisbury was also counted among the many witnesses to this bizarre phenomena during the summer of 1952. He described it as "about the size of a wash basin, usually at the height of an automobile headlight and about the same intensity."

Suddenly, it stopped as abruptly as it started even though older residents claimed it had been showing up periodically for half a century.

The *Salisbury Daily Times* featured a story, "Professor Believes Ghost Light Is Gas", in which a John Hopkins professor alleged the gas was being generated by decaying vegetable matter seeping to the surface and being moved around by a gust of wind. The professor stated, "It seems a shame to have state police out there all night trying to catch a little bag of gas."

The sightings apparently, according to some eyewitnesses, continued to occur off and on until after the road was blacktopped. The Wicomico County Road Division records the road being tarred and chipped in 1953, widened and rebuilt in 1958, and blacktopped in 1974. It may have been that dust from the old, original dirt road was reflected in automobile headlights providing the "Ghost Light Road" illusion.

Another more far-fetched theory was offered that included a broken shard of glass being carried into a low-hanging branch by a possum or raccoon. As cars would approach, they headlights would reflect into the glass, but just to a point before disappearing.

Local legend provides some other paranormal explanations, including that years ago when the railroad was being built, a man with a lantern was killed there and the light is his lantern. There is also a tale of a gambling dispute that resulted in a murder in this wooded area and the ghost of the murdered gambler haunts the road. Another legend states a black man was hung in the woods and left to die and it's his spirit that looks for the 'light of justice', and, finally, a local man committed suicide by hanging himself in the nearby forest and his body was never found until many years later.

I visited the site many years ago with some friends from a local bulletin board service, when those used to be quite popular. The road, properly called Old Railroad Road runs exactly two miles from U.S. Route 50 until it bends off sharply to the left and intersects with Main Street. The sightings were most often encountered between Portermill Road exactly one mile south of Route 50 and Church Street Extended, which is another half-mile south. I found it very interesting that even though the light had been inactive since the mid-1970s, a high-voltage power station was a quarter-mile further south of the actual sightings. While this may not mean anything, it might explain a lot.

MASSACHUSETTS

Raynham:
(Directions: SE Massachusetts along Rt. 138, Exit 8 off I-495)

A strange light has been seen over the railroad tracks that run beside the Raynham Dog Track. Besides the lights, unusual noises are sometimes heard in conjunction with the lights above the massive power lines that run through the swamp. Almost like clockwork, every January, 'spook lights' have been reported over the actual dog track. This area has been called "The Bridgewater Triangle" because of other strange events that occur here.

Sudbury:
(Directions: eastern Massachusetts along Rt. 27)

A ball of fire destroyed a barn on a farm near Sudbury, Massachusetts on April 28, 1965. It was witnessed from several different locations, and was generally described as a flaming basketball. No meteoric fragments were found and the case still remains a mystery.

MICHIGAN

Norway:
(Directions: upper peninsula Michigan on Rt. 2, E of Iron Mountain)
This story was related by Laurie Small from the Internet:

"Our home is in Michigan's Upper Peninsula, by a small town, called Norway. We live on a hardwood ridge, which is traversed by spring beds and the rivulets that come from them. The U.P. is a mostly rural area, with many acres of forests, wetlands, lakes, rivers and small farms. The residents are able to enjoy many outdoor sports, not the least of which are hunting and fishing.

"Being an avid hunter, I spent the hours from pre-dawn to after dusk during the firearm deer season (Nov. 15-30) afield, posting up for the hunt. We have enough property that I am able to hunt on what is virtually our backyard. It is not uncommon that during the time following dusk, a Light will appear on the ridge. At first, I blamed a neighbor or violator (someone who doesn't have permission to hunt on someone else's property) for the appearance of the Light. One time, I even called the neighbor across the field, asking if they had given anyone permission to hunt between us, and they had said they didn't. When we went to see if we could follow the tracks to determine where this 'violator' went, there were no tracks in the snow. Another time when I saw the Light from my deer blind, I checked the next day to see where the 'person' was posting and there was nary a track much less a blind to sit in. If this is a person, he has never fired his weapon (I have been living and hunting here for 16 years and would have surely heard a gun blast at such close range!) and he has never been seen coming or going.

"In November 1999, I had bagged a deer and dragged it back to our shed located in the yard by our house. I turned toward the woods and there was that same Light - sort of yellow in color with red around the edges. It was not the color of a fluorescent or halogen light and was hovering at the base of the top-most ridge. It lolled back and forth at about what I would estimate to be waist-height level. I went around the shed and stood in the shadow, watching it for almost 15 minutes. The light would wax and wane in size, like someone was turning slowly from front to side. After about 15 minutes the light moved from my view, and wondering if the wind was moving the trees so that my view was obscured, I took a few steps out from where I had been standing. I did not call out to the Light, but thinking it may be a person, had waited to see if he would move toward me. I again made visual contact with the Light and it then seemed to turn and began to follow the bottom of the ridge, traveling away from the house. All the while, it moved in a swaying motion as it moved away, finally disappearing after 150-200 yards.

"As this topic was brought up from time to time, I found out that quite a few of our neighbors have also seen this Light in the woods. As for myself, the Light does not make me feel uneasy or the least bit threatened. It has never approached any of our family and seem benign in nature. Our children have grown up seeing this Light in the woods and I suppose the children's theories on what the Light actually is (UFO guys), are as good as anyone else's guess. I know of no grisly horror story of murder or mayhem, and although I do believe that spirits can be among us, I don't feel that this is the case here.

"It was fascinating to read the theory that these lights may emanate from boggy, marshy land and are able to be blown with the wind. Through the length of our property are no less than four separate spring bed areas, which are located on the side of the ridge, some high up and some midway. These flow into a small, cedar swamp, and eventually make up a larger creek flowing off of our property. I have not seen our Light in the swamp, but consistently on the ridge where the spring beds are located. For what it's worth, these Lights appear irregardless as to if there is snow on the ground or not. I have not noticed them during the summer, but then again, I wasn't looking for them in the same intense manner as I look for things when I am hunting. I particularly enjoy that there are still mysteries in this world and that it gives up all something to contemplate."

Watersmeet:
(Directions: upper peninsula Michigan along Rt. 45, north of Rt. 2 near Collins Pond Road)

Ghost lights are not only a mystery to behold but sometimes are noted tourist attractions and the 'Mystery Light' seen between the towns of Watersmeet and Paulding in Michigan's Upper Peninsula is just that. The Watersmeet Business Directory flyer describes the light prominently on the back page:

"While in Watersmeet you should see 'The Mystery Light'.
"The 'Light' has defied explanation since it was first sighted about a dozen years ago, although theories abound. To observe the phenomenon, one must drive north from Watersmeet on U.S. 45 for four miles toward the neighboring village of Paulding, and take Robbins Lake Road for a short distance west - an unimproved rural lane once part of a military road authorized by Abraham Lincoln during the Civil War in anticipation of a

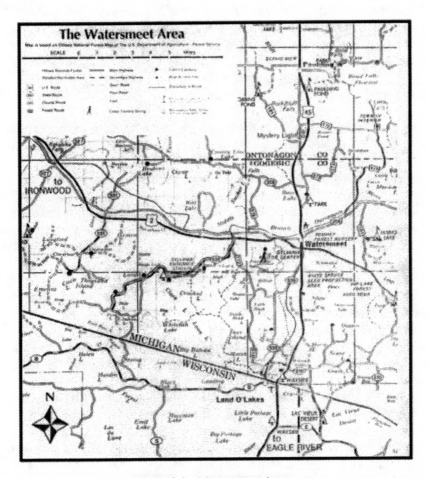

Map of the Watersmeet Area

British attack through Canada.

"By tramping through dense woods to the summit of nearby hills, the mysterious light can be observed almost every night once darkness has descended on the northern wilderness.

"It appears to rise slowly out of the forest and then hovers low in the sky for varying intervals - ranging from a couple of minutes to over a quarter of an hour. Often described as looking like a 'bright star' it first seems to be a campfire ember, reaching an intense reddish glow, then becoming a haze and finally receding to a mere spark before disappearing into the night.

"Explanations vary from fanciful to factual. Some say it's the spirit of a long dead mail carrier ambushed by Indians over a century ago; others insist it is the ghost of an engineer killed in a nearby railroad accident in years gone by. One woman thinks it's a mystical sign of religious significance.

"In the meantime, 'The Mystery Light' continues to baffle, intrigue and mystify the visitor."

The directions in the brochure are a little off though as local camping maps clearly mark the location with a little exploding ball of light in between U.S. 45 and old Highway 45, south of Route 172.

I first heard about the Watersmeet ghost light a number of years ago at a lecture in Chicago. The speaker said that the light was visible every night with very few exceptions and was a valid phenomenon. The next instance the light was brought to my attention was from a member of the *Ghost Research Society*, Bill Kingsley, who wrote an article about his encounters and included some amazing photographs!

"My impression was that these lights were alive......I feel that these lights are definitely not reflections from auto headlights or reflected light off of power line insulators. I feel that there is a natural explanation to these lights; but what?" said Kingsley.

Along with the article and photographs, he supplied two newspaper articles about the light. One from the *Detroit News* of January 26, 1982 and the other from the *Milwaukee Journal* of November 30, 1980.

"Some suspect the mystery lights have something to do with UFOs. A New Jersey UFO club checked it out but failed to confirm its suspicions," said James L. Kerwin in his *Detroit News* article.

Chris Roberts, a former Hazel Park, Illinois resident who operated a small general store at nearby Paulding, was quoted as saying, "People have made tests by having a friend blink their lights, on and off, going up the highway, but the mystery lights appear above their blinking headlights."

"Some say it's a ghost conductor killed in a train wreck many years ago, searching the tracks. Others think it may be a lost miner, looking for his claim. Then, the site is near old Military Road, to Fort Wilkins, where robbers killed a man delivering mail in 1870. They say the victim is looking for his dead sled dogs," says Bob Zelinski, who operates a canoe rental livery in neighboring Watersmeet.

Harry Pease of the *Milwaukee Journal* writes, "The snow was thinning. Zelinski got out a topographic map and pointed out the lay of the land. Sure enough, the mysterious lights in the woods are auto headlights and taillights on Highway 45. You pick them up on the long hill at Maple Grove Cemetery, eleven miles from Dingman's Rock. The cemetery lies about 1,315 feet above sea level. Paulding is down in a hole between there and the lookout points. The village puts a little glow in the sky - just enough to give the onlooker a false horizon."

Ripley's Believe It Or Not even offered in excess of $100,000 to the person or persons who could solve the mystery. There were no takers. The lights have been captured on film by *Michigan Magazine* and Channel Six News out of Marquette. Although some local people claim to have seen the strange lights over a long period of time, the first reported sighting was in 1966. A carload of teenagers had stopped one clear evening along a swampy area of the old Military Road called Dog Meadow. Suddenly, Rick Chiochios, the driver, reported a brilliance filled the car's interior and lit the power lines paralleling the road. The frightened young people fled to report their experience to the sheriff and since that time, many have witnessed the phenomenon, but none can explain it completely.

Joseph Ursitti, owner of the Running Bear Resort in Paulding, also explains how the power company failed to reveal the secret of the light. "They conducted a study of the light and said it could be the reflection of car lights on the electrical wires. They moved the wires three times but the light was always still visible, no matter what," Ursitti stated.

On a hot June evening in 1977, Elmer Lent and Harold Nowak of Wisconsin decided to check out the phenomenon. A newspaper account said that no sooner had they parked their car on the gravel road then the light appeared -- a bright spotlight shining directly at them. It moved closer, backed away, appeared at an angle from time to time. To Lent, who grew up in the shadow of a railroad yard, it looked like the headlight of a train. Suddenly, a smaller light appeared below the large light and slightly to the right. Lent recalled that 'the two, at times, seemed to move together, then apart, one or the other disappearing, then showing again.' The movements, he reasoned, were those a switchman would make in signaling with a lantern.

Sometimes the light changed color from white to red and occasionally a to a dim green. Lent judged the lights to be "two or three blocks away." After watching for an hour, Lent, still skeptical of any supernatural basis for the phenomenon, determined to catch the pranksters responsible. He and Nowak left the car and began walking. As they approached, the lights seemed to disappear down over the next rise but cast a bright glow in the sky.

A half-mile later, finding nothing that might explain the mystery, the pair turned around and the lights reappeared over the rise. When they reached their car, other observers said that, in the men's absence, they'd seen a large red light above a small white one in the middle of the road a block ahead of

Watersmeet Light Photographed by John Cachel

A close-up of the Light from the photo
above (Courtesy John Cachel)

them. These lights would have been between the men and their car. Two hours later, the men drove ahead for some distance, parked, and shut off the headlights. The lights reappeared, the large headlight and the smaller one beneath it beaming down the middle of the road. A minute later, the headlight vanished, and the smaller light, Lent said, "seemed to touch down and burst into three." The outer two lights disappeared, but the third remained, about two hundred feet away. Nowak snapped on the headlights but the light in the road didn't move. Then, several minutes later, it rose slowly to a height of four to five feet and vanished. Of his experience, Lent, still perplexed, said, "No teenagers, no flashlights, no strings attached."

With all this conflicting information and testimony I decided to check out the reports. I was joined by Richard Locke and Richard Kerscher, now deceased, of the *Ghost Research Society*. They volunteered to act as our guides and help with the investigation as they had both been to the Watersmeet area several times before and had witnessed the lights. Their conclusions were the lights were nothing more than automobile headlights and taillights seen from a distance and were nothing supernatural in nature.

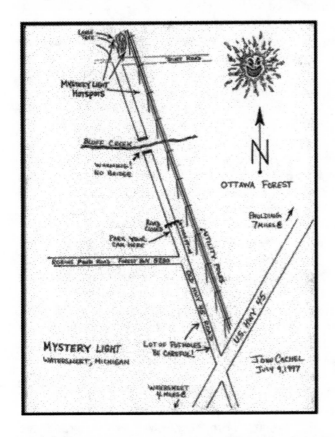

We all traveled to the area the week of September 13th through the 21st of 1986. Our first full day was spent trying to collect additional newspaper accounts, interview eyewitnesses and talk to various media contacts who might know something through reporting it. Most of our efforts were fruitless. Even the larger towns of Bessemer, Wakefield, Paulding and Bruce Crossing did not have any information that could be located.

Our first few nights observations were somewhat obscured by drizzle and haze but the light did make an appearance several times. We all saw both white and red lights as reported by Kingsley and many other reliable people, however we could not make a determination as to the cause of the appearances.

The following day was spent collecting topographic maps of the area and interviewing local forest rangers who knew the area well. We attempted to locate 'Dingman's Rock', which was mentioned in several newspaper articles as being the ideal viewing location without success. The name 'Dingman's Rock' is apparently local in origin and not listed on any surface or geographical survey maps of the region. We eventually located it, the night before we left for home.

That evening, we returned to the viewing area and were able to see the light quite clearly through high-power binoculars. It diffused very nicely into a pair of automobile headlights with an occasional taillight coming into view. However, I needed a bit more proof.

Next morning we traveled north beyond the viewing points along U.S. 45 toward Paulding. We located the small cemetery mentioned in the traveler's brochure and carefully plotted mileage from that point back to the observation points. We observed that the mileage is close to eleven miles as reported but perhaps less, since the point where the lights are first picked up are at the top of a large hill; elevation over 1,500 feet above sea level and nearly 200 feet higher than Maple Grove Cemetery. From that point, it's exactly 8.3 miles to Robbins Pond Road, which is also old Highway 45.

So what the observer is actually seeing are car lights topping the hill, occasionally dimming the high-beams for oncoming traffic, taillights of those oncoming cars passing the first cars, then their high-beams coming on again and then the cars finally disappearing into a deep slope in the road. By timing when the lights vanish from sight and when they pass behind you on U.S. 45 at an average speed of 55 miles per hour, it calculates to approximately seven minutes!

Stopwatch tests were performed to calculate the average amount of time the lights were in view at an average speed of 55 miles per hour and found this to be 90.2 seconds. By recreating the driving experience from the crest of the hill at 55 miles per hour for 90 seconds, we were relatively sure of the exact point on U.S. 45 where the mysterious lights vanish from view. From that point in the road, the observation point could no longer be seen.

On our last evening, we set up a video camera at the observation point and I had my brother, Wayne, drive down from the crest of the hill with the four-way flashers on. He was also instructed to blink the high-beams on and off every five seconds. The results were conclusive! We recorded the oncoming vehicle on tape flashing the brights every five seconds on cue! We had proved, beyond the shadow of a doubt, that the lights that visitors have been seeing for over twenty years were simply headlights and taillights and the terrain of the area, which causes them to disappear in a mysterious manner. I was elated however (predictably) the locals did not agree with our results.

MINNESOTA

Lake Shetek:
(Directions: Murray County, call Mn. Travel Line 800-657-3700)
Strange dancing lights and invisible footsteps pushing down the grass are thought to be caused by the spirits of Indians massacred by white settlers here in 'Slaughter Slough' in the mid-1800s. The Indians were buried under an earthen mound in an area that is now farmland.
(Source: National Directory of Haunted Places by Dennis William Hauck)

Old Brewery Spook Light:
(Directions: The small town of Le Seur, Minnesota is located in the south central part of the state, about fifty miles SW of Minneapolis/ St. Paul. Old Brewery Hill is located south of town along the road to Ottawa. The hill is located on the east side of the highway)
For many years local residents have seen a reddish ghost light dancing its way along the Omaha Railroad tracks just south of Le Seur. This area was once known as Old Brewery Hill because of the brewery that once graced this site back in 1875 and was built by George Kienzli. An old hermit was said to have lived in one of the old caves on the site of the former brewery, which burned down a number of years ago. He was seen exiting these caves at night by local folk often carrying a lantern. The man died long ago but residents still see the ghostly red light from his lantern gracing the tracks from time to time.
(Source: Ghosts of the Prairie Website - www.prairieghosts.com)

MISSISSIPPI

Flag Stop:
(Directions: near Beauregard which is 40 miles S of Jackson on US Hwy 51, 2 miles N of the Wesson exit on I-55)
For many years along the Illinois Central railroad tracks here, a phantom man has tried to stop trains by swinging a spectral light back and forth. The first encounter was in 1926, when a train heading for McComb was flagged down by a man with a lantern. When the engineer and brakeman searched the area for the flagman, no one could be found. This area became known as "Flag Stop" by trainmen and the sightings continued for years. It is not known

if the spectral light is still seen today.

MISSOURI

<u>El Dorado Springs:</u>
(Directions: near Blackjack on Rt. 82, N of US Hwy 54)

A single light was reported flickering along the Sac River near El Dorado Springs late in March 1959. Some eyewitnesses reported the light was red, changing to white and green.

A man by the name of Duane Witt, who worked in a print shop in El Dorado Springs, said he saw the light four times during March. He said it was near Blackjack, approximately ten miles east of El Dorado Springs. Witt and some of his friends chased it around a field. They said it looked to be about the size of a football, but they couldn't get closer than about a block away.

"It just seems to bob and drift away," Witt said. "Somebody is out chasing it almost every night. One night we counted forty cars lined up along the road leading by that field."

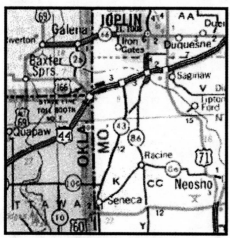
The Spooklight Area

<u>Joplin:</u>
(Directions: from Joplin - I-44 west, State Rd. 43 south, Road BB west, right at T-intersection, first road on the left)

Perhaps one of the most famous ghost lights ever reported, it's been called by many names, including The Tri-State Spooklight, and many neighboring communities claim the light as their own such as Neosho, Joplin, Hornet, Quapaw and Seneca. Allegedly first encountered during the infamous Trail Of Tears in 1836, the light was officially first reported in 1881, according to a publication published by Foster Young entitled *Ozark Spooklight*. However, in 1896 the small hamlet of Hornet was rocked by numerous sightings a large ball of light seen moving through the fields.

The Spooklight is actually seen and encountered in Oklahoma near the town of Quapaw, because the best viewing point is on the Missouri-Oklahoma border and the light is truly in the state of Oklahoma and hasn't made many treks into the state of Missouri.

"I don't really know what it is, and I hope they never find out, it would spoil the mystery," said Joe Smith, a gregarious man who is president of the Bank of Quapaw and having spent all of his 77 years in the area.

"It's kind of a legend around here, and it's been forever that

Photo of the Spooklight by Marta Churchwell of the *Joplin Globe*

people have gone out to look for it," says Suzanne J. Wilson, a local writer. "I've only seen it in the distance....but I've seen it."

Noel Grisham, who lives a mile or so off Spooklight Road, thinks maybe he's seen it, too. But he's more skeptical. "It could be a flashlight for all I know," he says. "But when the weather's nice and you're sitting out in the yard at night, you'll get five or ten people a week pulling up hollering at you," Grisham says, "They're holler, 'Is this where the Spooklight is? We want to see Spooklight.'"

Legends are many for the possible cause, including one of the oldest handed down by the Quapaw Indians who live nearby. They tell of two young Indian lovers who wished to marry but the chief demanded an unusually large amount for his daughters hand. Unable to meet his demand, they decided to elope against the chief's wishes. A war party was soon dispatched once the two were discovered missing. They both knew if they were captured, the punishment would be harsh for their deed and they decided to commit suicide by leaping together from the top of a high bluff overlooking nearby Spring River. The light that is now seen is said to be the spirits of the young lovers brought together by death.

In the 1870 era, another legend told of a miner whose cabin was raided by Indians while he was away. His wife and children were taken captive and he never saw them again. He is allegedly still searching for them with his lantern.

One of the local ministers, who belongs to a fundamentalist congregation from the area, was quoted as saying that he believes the strange light is some form of evil spirit of the type that might have been cast out by Jesus Christ in several stories from the Bible. He goes on to say that this evil spirit has become trapped at this location for some inexplicable reason. Another member of the clergy simply has a totally different explanation for the phenomenon. He believes the light is a sign of the imminent return of our Lord, Jesus Christ. He frequently quotes the New Testament in several passages and mentions "signs and wonders" that will precede him.

One of the most interesting explanations of the phenomenon is that the Spooklight marks the spot where a group of Cherokee Indians, racked by hunger, disease and exhaustion, were forced to sell their women into slavery near the end of the long and torturous Trail of Tears of 1836. According to the legend, the Spooklight glows as an eternal reminder of the cruelty and inhumanity of the forced evacuation of the Indians from their homeland to the reservations.

And, of course, there is a legend concerning a farmer who was captured by Indians and beheaded. His lantern light is still seen along the road looking for his disembodied head!

But there is yet another possible paranormal explanation for the light. Back when highway construction workers were laying and carving out the Spooklight road, they supposedly cut right through sacred Indian burial grounds and desecrated many grave sites. In fact, some skeletal remains were unearthed and strewn about. Perhaps those disturbed from their eternal rest are now still haunting this section of road in anger and confusion.

June Smith is the senior reference librarian at the Joplin Public Library, 20 miles to the northwest. Like so many others, she has her own Spooklight theory. "I've always figured it was an accumulation of gases, and you saw it when the time was right," she said. "Nobody has ever really figured out the reason for it.....During World War II, the Army Corps of Engineers even had people down here looking."

It was around that time that Mrs. Smith was transformed from Spooklight skeptic to Spooklight believer. She was getting ready to return home with her 2-year-old daughter and friends after a fruitless night of Spooklight watching. "We had two carloads down there and we hadn't seen anything," she said. "And I thought, well, I don't believe it anyway. And then here it came down the road.

"It looked like the size of a basketball, and as it came toward you, it got larger. By the time it got to the second car it almost exploded. It was the size

Map of the Joplin Spooklight Area

of the second car."

One local Kansas City, Missouri researcher believes that most of the time the lights are nothing more than refracted headlights from Interstate 44 caused by water vapors from the Spring River. But every ten years or so, the real Spooklight appears in the form of ball lightning.

Keith Partain, a Tulsa researcher, who holds degrees in entomology and zoology developed his own theory in 1986, "When you see a little wriggle at the end of the road, it's one car following another on a distant road."

Whatever it is, this elusive light has been appearing along a section of a road known as the "Devil's Promenade" since around 1881, long before there were any automobiles around to possibly cause it to be mistaken for headlights or reflections of headlights considering the Route 66 extension was completed in 1934. It has baffled researchers, scientists and investigators ever since.

From the very first recorded episodes of the light, in the early 1880s, it seemed to have a great deal of freedom of movement. Homesteaders, settlers and residents of the area frequently experienced the light over a fairly large area. It appeared to wander and drift about almost at random for several miles in every direction.

The local expert at the time we began our research into the spooklight was Garland "Spooky" Middleton, now deceased, who once owned a small building at the edge of the Missouri-Oklahoma border. This building was converted into a Spooklight Museum where Spooky would entertain both locals and out-of-state visitors to the area with ice-cold soda and tales of the spooklight through the years. The museum housed the best collection of pictures and newspaper articles concerning the light to date.

In the early years of this establishment, Spooky used to have binoculars and telescopes set up, facing the road, and for ten cents a peek, you could look for the light.

The Old Spooklight Museum near the Viewing Area

Unfortunately, after the death of Spooky, the building the area was bought up by new residents who did not share the same enthusiasm for the light that ol' Spooky did. They closed down the museum and actually tried to deter visitors to the site for a time.

Garland "Spooky" Middleton outside of the Spooklight Museum

I do remember interviewing Spooky at great length about the more impressive encounters with the Spooklight. He pointed to a nearby field within a hundred yards or so and recalled an eerie encounter that he had one evening. He remembered that the spooklight appeared on the road just after sunset and began to roll like a basketball giving off sparks as it tumbled down the gravel road. It then entered into a grassy field where several cows were quietly grazing away. It appeared to move silently among the cattle without disturbing them one bit! In fact, the animals paid no attention to there illuminated visitor at all!

Louise Graham of Galena, Kansas described her encounter while a passenger on a school bus traveling through the area. "While coming home from a school carnival at Quapaw, Oklahoma, we got the thrill of our lives. The light had evidently grown tired and weary and decided to do a little hitchhiking on our bus. The light perched on the rear window as though trying to get in the bus. We were scared half to death - women screaming and all. The light was so bright it temporarily blinded the bus driver and he had to stop the bus. Just as we stopped, the light went away. I'll never forget that bus ride."

The spooklight has the tendency to creep up on teenagers who park in this area with their girlfriends. The dark road is a haven for lovers and beer drinkers, as well Spooklight investigators. This pattern of the light sneaking up on unsuspecting parkers seems to date back as far as the 1880s since it was reported during horse and buggy days. Some of the earliest homesteaders complained that the light would suddenly in the windows of their homes during their most private moments. Others reported the light actually invading their homes when first spotted.

The light would then subdivide into multiple lights, according to eyewitness accounts, sometimes numbering as many as six or seven separate smaller lights. The lights would then begin to change color rapidly and dance around the room in a mad frenzy. Then, they would make a dash for the doors and windows and exit through them without a sound and disappear.

A farfetched theory about the light has been proposed by several investigators, including Bob Loftin, who I will discuss in detail a bit later. Could the light that is seen and has been seen by thousands of people actually be a UFO? There have been numerous daylight UFO photographs taken over the vicinity in the past. Could this area be a landing zone for extraterrestrial spacecraft?

The very first recorded investigation of the Spooklight was in 1942 by a group of students from the University of Michigan. They set up campsites in the area for about two weeks and began testing and experimenting to determine it's origin and causes. Allegedly, they even shot at the light with high-powered rifles. They recalled that the light only blinked out for a second or two and then reappeared at the same location. They came away completely mystified and without any answers.

Next, the United States Army Corp of Engineers from nearby Camp Crowder began their research and studies of the phenomena in 1946. They used every type of experiment known, including the use of signal lights on a road thirteen miles away, trying to prove that car lights were the source of the ghost light. They made no definitive conclusion. However, Captain R.L. Loftin later believed the engineers had used the wrong road.

This statement is most interesting because of the confusion of the roads. I personally interviewed residents of the area concerning the Spooklight in it's earlier days. The light that now appears on the Devil's Promenade is not where it was first observed. The actual road where initial reports surfaced is exactly one mile north of the current road site. This is the road where the Army Corp of Engineers conducted their experiments.

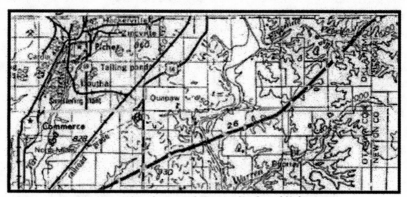

A topographical map of the Joplin Spooklight Area

Later, for some reason, the light moved to it's current location, one mile to the south. This is where it is always seen now. Residents of the area believe that the light displays some form of intelligence and, perhaps, sensing the other road was becoming overcrowded with new homesteads, decided to move to the other less inhabited roadway.

Captain Loftin experimented with spotlights on Highway 66 and was sure the headlight theory was accurate, however I disagree. He described a high ridge between the ghost light and the highways and believed that the density and rarity of the atmosphere as it rises over the ridge causes the light to bend and act the way it does.

This does not explain the fact that the light was seen before the development of the automobile nor does it take into consideration that the atmospheric anomalies he spoke of would only occur under special conditions. The ghost light can be seen virtually any night from dusk to dawn and under a number of different weather conditions.

"The test....has no connection whatsoever with the present spook lights. The army test was conducted on a road approximately one mile north of the road from which the light is seen today. The result of this test has been best described by the State of Missouri, Resources and Development Division stating...'They came away baffled.' The tri-pod mounted telescope, now operated on the new spook light road, Courtesy of Spooksville, is three times more powerful than those used by the army. The light as seen through this scope cannot be separated into a pair or pairs of automobile headlights. The light as seen through the telescope appears as a fiery flame or flames, usually green at the bottom and red at the top. It is sure worth seeing," related Loftin in a small book entitled *Ghost Lights*.

In January of 1983, I wrote to the Tulsa District Corps of Engineers in a hope to gain more insight into the investigation. This is the response that I received, "The Tulsa District of the Corps of Engineers has never made any investigation of the Spooklight near Joplin, Missouri. The Joplin area was, at one time, part of the area included in the Tulsa District's boundary but no study or investigation of the light was ever made," said John O. Thistler, Chief, Public Affairs Office. Hmmmm!

A high school student, a few years later, made a study of the light using colored signals, etc. An automobile with red cellophane over the headlights was driven on the Quapaw Highway and the student, William E. Underwood, stationed at the Spook Light site, took colored films of the refracted lights. His tests and conclusions merely repeated those of Dr. Ward and Captain Loftin.

Around 1945, Dr. George W. Ward, formerly of the National Bureau of Standards, made some first-hand observations of the phenomena and basically said, about the headlight theory, that "the relative humidity and temperature would have to attain the correct values to produce the correct density of atmosphere to bend the light sufficiently for observation."

In a letter to Loftin, Ward writes: "Following our telephone conversation this weekend, I am relating my first experience regarding the "Spook Light," near Hornet, including the refraction theory, which you have received. It has been a pleasure working with you and I wish you every success in your publication.

"I came to Kansas City, January 1945, from the National Bureau of Standards, Washington, D.C., to aid in the development of the Midwest Research Institute. Part of this effort involved addresses to various groups such as Chambers of Commerce, Rotary, etc. It was while appearing in Joplin that one of the Joplin newspaper reporters recounted the story of the "Spook Light" or as he called it, the "Mysterious Light of the Ozarks." Naturally, being trained scientifically, my curiosity was aroused. Arrangements were immediately made with the Joplin newspaper reporter, whose name I have forgotten momentarily, to view the phenomenon.

"We drove down south of Joplin some eight to ten miles and eventually parked on a gravel road at the top of a long slope, the road continuing down hill away from us, as we faced west, to dissipate itself in a number of cattle paths. The moon was not up and our reporter friend claimed that the night was ideal for observation.

"Not long after our arrival, a suffused glow appeared in the sky, to the west over a range of hills, the center of the lighted area being in line with the axis of the road. This was followed almost immediately by a ball of light estimated as four to six feet in diameter that appeared to descend out of the hills and to rapidly advance toward us.

"As the greenish-yellow ball of light approached, the Publicity Director of the Institute caused some amusement by exclaiming that he had seen enough and he dashed back to lock himself in the car. The light approached and seemed to envelop us. Upon rapidly turning toward the east to observe the continuance of the light past us I observed nothing.

"After observing the phenomenon a second time, I placed an observer at these points, one in the center of the road, another some fifty feet behind him and one at the fence line on each side of the road. I was the first observer on the road and found that after the light passed me I could not see it, but that the observer 50 feet to my rear could still see it. The fence line observers reported only an obscure flash appearance. These observations then caused me to believe that the source of the phenomenon lay ahead to the west and preferably over the range of hills. Further reasoning led to the possibility that the cause lay in the refraction of automobile headlights from a road in direct line with the gravel road where we stood. The fact that the light did not always appear, substantiated the refraction or bending of light idea in that the relative humidity and temperature would have to produce the correct density of atmosphere to bend the light sufficiently for observation. Further it was observed that as an observer moved down hill toward the observed source of light, the phenomenon was not visible while an observer remaining at approximately the top of the slope could see the light. The refraction theory was also borne out by the lack of good observation at the fence lines.

"Satisfied that we were dealing with the refraction of distant automobile headlights - one light instead of two, automatically called for distance - we sought on the highway road map a road traveled by cars that was directly in line with our observation point. It was decided that such a road was the section of highway running east and west from Commerce to Quapaw, Oklahoma.

"It now remained to correlate automobile headlights on the highway with observation of the 'Spook Light.' We had satisfied ourselves as to the probable explanation and had no further interest. We suggested observation from an airplane as to cars in Oklahoma and a radio report to a ground observer of the 'Spook Light.'

"We were quite pleased at your offer to collaborate when you learned of our theory. Your experiments with lights on the aforementioned highway was followed with a good deal of interest. It was indeed most gratifying when you finally proved our theory."

Vance Randolph, writer on Ozark folkways, mentioned the light in his *Ozark Superstitions*, published in 1947. He had seen the light on three separate occasions and remarked that at first it looked to be about the size of an egg, but later seemed to be as large as a "washtub". He mentioned that it was a single glow.

In the Fall of 1955, a group of students from Shawnee Mission, Kansas High School, including; Albert Yeomen, Phil Hennessey, Simpson Yeomen, Bob Keeley, John DuBois, Mike O'Keefe, Bill Calvin and Larry Scamon, looked into the light. The group was assisted in experiments by Loftin.

They came equipped with cameras, electronic measuring devices and communication equipment. They tested mines in the area for strange gases, atmospheric electricity and car lights. No concrete answers were found.

One geologist theorized that the Spooklight might be some kind of "electrical emanation from ore beneath the ground." In other words, some form of piezoelectric effect. Another individual looked through binoculars and was sure that it was a light on top of a gravel pile

Also in1955, a civil engineer, Richard Y. Jones conducted a test along with the late Charles W. Graham of the *Kansas City Star*. They brought along to the site a surveyor's transit and when the light appeared they looked through the transit and discovered two lights, side by side, similar to automobile headlights. They also had cars drive both east and west along Route 66, flashing their lights and it was noted that these were seen along certain points of the spooklight road. beyond Quapaw!

Robert Gannon of *Popular Mechanics* conducted a similar test in 1965 accompanied by Dr. Henry H. Hicks and Jean Prideaux. Henry H. Hicks, professor of mechanical engineering at the University of Arkansas, also observed the light and said, "I rather doubt that atmospheric refractions could cause the effect (because) refractions are subdued at night..." and, he adds, that in his opinion, the light is "some kind of fixed light, perhaps a billboard light, (but) some of the mechanisms are not clear."

A billboard light? Seen since 1881? A light miles away but clear enough to be fixed on top of a gravel pile? Headlights? Refractions? Numerous explanations abound.

Jean Prideaux, an instructor in mechanical engineering, with a specialty in fluid dynamics arrived at the site with a sixty-power telescope constructed by Prof. Hicks. According to the observation, the light or lights resolved themselves as car lights through the telescope.

There is conflicting information on the actual elevation of the Spooklight road. The Loftin report says the road slopes away from you towards the reported light. I believe this might be the wrong road, in other words, the road exactly one mile north from the present spook light sightings. Another researcher says there is a large slope towards the middle of the road and it then rises towards the end. While my research indicates the elevation varies from 895 to 1067 feet while Interstate 44 ranges from 813 to 882 feet, which, if true, would indicate that the highest point of the interstate is still below the lowest point of the spooklight road. Therefore you couldn't physically see the lights thru solid earth and they would have to be refracted for all to see every night!

John W. Northrip, a professor of physics and astronomy at Southwest Missouri State University, didn't believe in the spooklight at all. Northrip and some of his students proved that rising heat from surrounding hills was carrying light from a nearby highway and giving it its spooklight appearance, making it dance and hover.

In the late 1960s, Dr. Robert H. Gibbons utilized a laser to determine that headlights seen from Highway 66 could be mistaken for the notorious light. He admitted, however, that such tests do not rule out the possible existence of the Spooklight.

"The test we conducted back in the '60s did prove you could see lights from the highway, but there are also the stories of it approaching people and burning cars. It may possibly be something else, like ball lightning. I've become a little more open-minded about it since then."

Gibbons had also managed to capture the spooklight on film and videotape, as have others through the years. When the crew from *Real People* arrived to produce a segment on the spooklight in the spring of 1981, footage taken by Gibbons was used when television cameras failed to pick up the image of the spooklight. The segment was aired nationally in December of the same year.

During Labor Day weekend in 1982, *Ghost Research Society* members traveled to Joplin to conduct our own investigations and first-hand observations of the spooklight. We, quite literally, chased this elusive light up and down the road from dusk to dawn never able to get close to identify it. We were able to get several excellent photographs and saw the image through 10x50 binoculars.

We observed it the best after three in the morning when the traffic on the actual road ceased to be a problem. Two other *GRS* members and myself were stalking the light as quietly as possible when suddenly I was able to see the light a few feet above the ground and near a distant barn. At first

Photo of the Joplin Spooklight Taken during the 1982 GRS investigations

glance, I thought the barn was on fire or perhaps someone had a bonfire raging nearby, because it was so extremely bright! It was at this point of time that I entered into what I would later call "a zone of fear" taken from the mentioned John Keel book. It was like a sudden, uncontrollable panic attack but also something I have not experienced there since.

All I wanted to do was run for the car and drive away but my curiosity got the best of me and I plunged forward, finally exiting this mysterious zone. At that point, I was approximately seventy-five to a hundred yards away and was in for the shock of my life, at least to that point. The light did not appear to be a simple ball but a diamond-shaped object with a hollow center and a golden hue. We could actually see the trees and bushes right through the empty center of this object. My other researchers later verified the sighting upon my return to the car.

It stayed in that relative position for about thirty seconds and then disappeared slowly behind a hill. What was truly remarkable was the space that was just occupied a moment ago by this light, now twinkled and glowed with some form of luminosity or phosphorescence. It quite literally sparkled with energy!

It then reappeared in that same location twice more, bobbing up and down like a fisherman's cork on the water, before disappearing altogether. We crept silently up the hill in the car hoping to see where it had gone. But before we got to the crest of the hill, it suddenly reappeared right in the middle of the road ahead of us less than seventy yards away! The light then proceeded to perform the now famous 'bobbing action' before disappearing after the third appearance. We attempted to crest the hill as quickly as possible but as we reached the summit, the light was already an estimated mile and a half away in the distance treetops. Total elapsed time to arrive at the summit was no more than sixty seconds!

During that same weekend I personally interviewed more than a dozen witnesses who supplied me with most interesting stories. One in particular was almost too good to be true. Between ten to fifteen people observed the light as close as thirty feet distance! They said the light was about the size of a basketball, orange-yellow in color, throbbing and slowly rolling along the ground. They were not frightened but awestruck and remained extremely quiet. Suddenly, some cars behind them began to crunch the gravel on the road, attempting to obtain a closer and better view.

The light was said to rise up about ten to twelve feet above the ground, split into two sections and shoot into the woods in either direction. A series of black and white photographs taken by Marta Churchwell of the *Joplin Globe* show the light performing a similar trick. A large bright ball is seen in the center of the photograph and then a long streak of white light moved quickly to the left as though it was moving quickly to the left and away from the photographer.

The *GRS* returned again in May of 1983 with more personnel and lots of new equipment. We brought along infrared film and a four and a half inch reflector telescope with a camera-mount. However, inclement weather hampered our chances of deploying the telescope and getting a much better picture of the orb. Using the 35mm cameras and time exposures lasting from thirty to ninety seconds, we did capture what appeared to be an extremely bright star and several shots showing distinct movement and separation into many sections. Some pictures show the light splitting into two or three parts. Others show side to side motion.

We were able to capture the light on video tape and the footage is quite remarkable! The tape is clear enough to show the background, which is useful for gauging distance and size as well as other stationary street lights in the distance. The Spooklight is clearly visible in the film and appears to move about, glows brighter and dimmer from time to time and disappears in a most unusual fashion. Instead of simply extinguishing itself altogether quickly, the light begins to dim considerably and slowly fades out like a campfire that is beginning to drown out. In fact, the light is reminiscent of a candle flame seen from several miles away!

We have since returned numerous times to view, investigate and record the light. It's always there for all to see and inspire. On NBC's *The Other Side* I was asked to investigate the light for television along with Sheri Sanders, the local NBC affiliate anchor. Of all the times I visited the site, this was the only time it failed to make an appearance. I blame this no-show on several factors.

First, we weren't at the proper viewing point for the light to be visible and with all the portable camera lights, technicians, curious onlookers and excitement, no wonder the light was hesitant about making an appearance. Wouldn't you be?

One of the most thorough investigations of the light was conducted by members of the *Ghost Research Society* in June 2002 using the latest in high technology.

Topographical and hand-drawn maps of the area were employed along with high-powered binoculars, 35mm cameras with telephoto lens, Sony Nightshot cameras, Magnetometers, Geiger counters, Negative Ion Detectors and CB radios.

The GRS crew for the 2002 Investigations. (Left to Right): Jim Graczyk, Stan Suho, Howard Hight, Ruth Kaczmarek, Donna Boonstra & Virginia Hight (Photo by Dale Kaczmarek)

Upon our arrival, we gathered additional information from various sources throughout the Joplin area and even appeared on NBC affiliate station KSN on our first night of observation. The team included GRS members Donna Boonstra, Jim Graczyk, Stan Suho, Howard and Virginia Hight, my wife, Ruth Kaczmarek, and myself.

A stationary command post was set up near the intersection of Stateline Road and the Spooklight road, while two other outposts were stationed further down the road at various intervals. Each command post was equipped with cameras, binoculars, maps, and CB radios for reporting their individual observations back to the Command Post.

Partly due to the television coverage our first night there, traffic along the road was increased as locals came out to see what our team was up to and to relate their personal experiences of the light. Many had some interesting tales to tell including an uncle of one person who described his encounter with the light in 1930. He claimed to have seen the light float across the road and into an adjacent field, slam into the ground and break up into a thousand pieces of small individually lit lights!

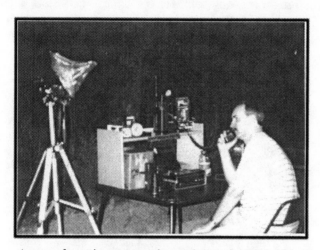

A scene from the command post during the 2002 GRS Investigation of the Joplin Spooklight

The first two nights went by without a single report from any of our outposts, or the Command Post, about any activity, even though others coming from further down the road claimed to have seen it. Constantly hampered by a bright full moon, we decided on our last night of observation to go completely mobile and abandon the Command Post idea. This is where our expedition hit pay dirt.

Further down the road, in what I call "The Hollow" or "Zone of Fear", we began to make observations of a single light well above the elevation of the road and inconsistent of headlight color or proximity to the ground. These sightings continued throughout the evening and early morning hours, even though traffic was now at a bare minimum. Obviously what we were seeing was not other car headlights and, at one point, we were so close to the interstate that you could even hear the large trucks rolling by, but could not see any reflections or direct images of car headlights on the interstate. We could hear them, but could not see them or even the interstate road, for that matter.

We were unable to photograph the light, but believe we did videotape several seconds of a most unusual light formation, which was definitely not a headlight of an approaching car.

We do plan on yet another investigation of the light, perhaps as early as 2003, and we have learned that we need to be more mobile and perhaps even incognito when it comes to the media, at least until we are almost ready to head back home! Also, included in the future planning of this investigation would be the lunar implications and attempting to view the light with no moon at all. This would be the ideal condition.

I would like to leave you with this thought concerning the spooklight. I showed some photographs to Pat Shenburg, former president of the Illinois Society for Psychic Research and a highly-gifted clairvoyant, with whom I have worked with many times. After she examined the pictures and I explained our sighting of the diamond-shaped object with a hollow center she said, "The light isn't a light but a doorway to another dimension." She insisted that I was in great danger while I was there. Who knows.... perhaps everyone might be?

Knob Noster:
(Directions: Johnson County at intersection of US Hwy 50 and Hwy 23)

The ghost of a hermit who lived on the top of a hill here returns during stormy weather. The man died mysteriously, some say of fright, during a violent thunderstorm. He was on his way down the hill to seek shelter in town and his body was found lying next to his lantern, which was still burning. Now his ghost, still carrying the lantern, is seen coming down the path into town whenever thunderstorms rage through the area. Locally known as the "Hermit Light."

(Source: National Directory of Haunted Places by Dennis William Hauck)

Northview:
(Directions: off I-44 between Northview & Marshfield, in Webster County)

Strange lights began glowing off Interstate 44 between Northview and Marshfield in rural Webster County in the Ozark Mountains in December 1991, drawing hundreds of watchers and creating traffic hazards. Mysterious, almost surgical mutilations of at least eleven cattle began the same time, and some speculate the lights and killings were connected.

(Source: Atlas of the Mysterious in North America by Rosemary Ellen Guiley)

Senath Light:
(Directions: located in Arbyrd in extreme SW Missouri along Hwy 108 just N of Hwy 164)

The location is in the river bottoms along an abandoned rail line and is known as the Senath Light. Getting there requires driving through miles and miles of desolate farm country on narrow blacktop roads. Then, you have to turn off on a gravel road that soon turns to a dirt track. Eventually you can see the built up rail road bed, up ahead and sweeping out of sight to the north.

Supposedly, a train conductor had fallen off a train and was decapitated and the light was the conductor still looking for his head, swinging his lantern along the track. Others say that it was the light of the old train, like a ghost train. And still another legend of the light around here is that the light is a ghost of a woman carrying a lantern up and down the road looking for her husband. He was said to have been hanged in a nearby tree. A fourth legend states this is where three sisters burned inside their home, while the oldest was waiting for her boyfriend to come for her. She apparently had a lantern in the window to let him know that it was all right for him to come by. The lantern allegedly caught the curtains on fire when they all fell asleep. The boyfriend never came and the three burned in the house. To this day, it is said that on the anniversary of that fateful night you will see the light of the lantern roaming the area in a search for the boyfriend that never showed.

One couple who came here shut off their car, flashed their headlights 3 times (again according to local legend) and waited. After about 30 minutes they saw what appeared to be a car approaching. It was probably a 1\4 of a mile from them when they realized it was only one light. It was some distance back, then all of a sudden it jumped towards them, then backed off, then it was coming back again. The driver decided to drive into the light -- then it just disappeared.

MONTANA

Grassrange:
(Directions: on US Hwy 19, 30 miles E of Lewistown)

These mysterious lights were first reported as early as 1881. In fact, there is an article in Helena's *Daily Herald*, dated March 23, 1881, which was entitled "Ghostly Visitations!" Lights had been seen moving around the farm of the late Charles Tacke, who was killed by Peter Pelkey. The murderer was hanged for his crime but residents said that the lights were most likely the spirits of the two men not entirely at rest.

The light appeared to be that of a red lantern and upwards of four were seen at one time dancing about and elevating to a height of over twenty feet above the ground! According to one eyewitness, the orb was "apparently from four to six inches in diameter and from eighteen to twenty-four inches high, the body of the light being of an orange color, occasionally flashing off rays of a greenish or sometimes of a bluish tintage, to a distance of forty to fifty feet."

Kalispell:
(Directions: located in western Montana along Hwy 93 and Hwy 2)

A most unusual light with colors ranging from yellow to green to purple was seen by many persons. Apparently first seen on Sunday, February 8, 1959, it was never satisfactorily explained. It is probably inactive today.

NEVADA

Gardenerville:
(Directions: extreme SW Nevada along Rt. 206 S of Carson City)

A Mrs. Sara Elizabeth Lampe of Gardenerville actually watched the formation of a light in the snow one early morning. In her account, written in 1951, Mrs. Lampe states that she and her husband lived along on an isolated ranch in Nye County. Early on a January morning in 1949, after a heavy snowfall, she awakened and was looking out a window at the white landscape dimly illuminated by the moon. She continues:

"Gradually, my eyes focused upon a pale gray stain, irregularly shaped and no bigger than my two hands. It rested on the smooth crust....about three rods from the house and in line with the window. Almost at once this fuzzy-gray shadow that was not a shadow bloomed into a disc of clear white light approximately three feet in diameter. It lay there for fully two minutes. Then suddenly contracting into a brilliant orange-tinted stream five or six inches wide, flowed swiftly over the snow toward my window and, to all appearances, exploded soundlessly against the stone foundation of the intervening front porch.

"Several tongues of scintillating red-and-blue flame spurted a few inches above the two-and-a-half foot high wainscoting of the porch. That was all. When daylight came, we searched conscientiously but found no signs, marks, or tracks of any kind that might help to explain the phenomenon."

(Courtesy of: *Mysterious Fires and Lights* by Vincent H. Gaddis)

King's River Ranch:
These lights have been seen by hundreds of people, and are similar in form and actions to those of the Oregon Canyon Ranch.

One outstanding example of a close encounter with the strange lights comes from William Bathlot, who was a homesteader in Beaver County,

Oklahoma. One evening in 1905, Bathlot and a hired hand were out searching for a lost cow and Bathlot was carrying his double-barreled shotgun. Suddenly, a ball of light appeared directly in front of the two startled men. They tried to walk around it, but it cut off all their movement. When they moved toward the light, it retreated, and when they stepped back, it followed. Then, as Mr. Bathlot later recounted.

"We just stood there with that thing about a dozen feet in front of us, silent as death itself. It was transparent. We could see a bunch of sagebrush right through its body. We could see no body resembling bird or animal, nor could we see anything resembling legs to hold it up. It was just a ball of light. Yet apparently this strange object could see us, and it checked our every move. The deadly unnerving stillness of the thing seemed to paralyze us. Finally, I raised my shotgun to my shoulders and let it have both barrels. The light went out."

Bathlot and his hired hand could find no trace of blood or other substance on the ground. Bathlot's experience should have been enough for a lifetime, but in 1950, an elderly William Bathlot paid a return visit to Oklahoma to see relatives. While there, a car in which he was riding was followed for a short distance by two lights!

McDermitt:
(Directions: extreme northern Nevada along US Hwy 95)

Near McDermitt, Nevada, is the Oregon Canyon Ranch and its famous lights. These lights are scattered over the entire ranch and do not have any periodic schedule for appearances, but are seen quite often by the ranch hands and herders. The area is quite high - over 4,000 feet above sea level - and dry. The lights are about the size of an automobile headlight, and are usually red or yellow in color. They share the trait of vanishing when approached, although they have been known to follow observers. There are reports of cowboys following the lights on their frightened horses for several miles.

NEW JERSEY

Lake Wanaque:
Multiple moving have been seen in the hills to the west.

(Source: Atlas of the Mysterious in North America by Rosemary Ellen Guiley)

Morris County:

The Vestigia Research team, a volunteer group interested in unexplained phenomenon, set up camp on the railroad tracks in the hills of Morris County, New Jersey. The train schedule was suspended for the night.

Forming two groups, the research chemists, electronic engineers and computer specialists, set up their cameras, telescopes, magnetometers, oscilloscopes, and other instruments at one check point. A second check point was established approximately one mile down the arrow-straight section of track on a cold November night in 1976, with snow underfoot.

These check points maintained contact with the team leaders using portable radios. Over 4,000 feet of fine wire was laid in between the rails to detect any electrical frequency that might be present. The wire was attached to an amplifier and oscilloscope. Other wires, attached directly to the rails, would measure the capacitance that existed between them. The other sensing equipment was a Geiger counter, compass, thermometers, infrared sensors, methane gas detectors, a radar unit, barometer and a parabolic microphone.

At 10:21 p.m., Post 2 made a sighting. They radioed to their friends and were amazed to find they saw nothing, although both groups had the same line of sight. The light was about 300-400 feet from their check point. The other posts scanned the area with radar and binoculars but could detect anything. The light remained visible for one minute, thirty-five seconds. At first it appeared on one side of the tracks, but moved over and positioned itself directly above the tracks and began to sway from side-to-side. The estimates indicate the object was from three to six inches in diameter. When it disappeared, it did so suddenly and did not fade away slowly.

The oscilloscope gave a reading of around 40,000 hertz and the capacitance test showed something shorting the two rails, as if a wire had been laid across them. Nine minutes after the light disappeared, the Geiger counter gave a full-scale reading for ten seconds and then registered normal background radiation, followed by another full-scale reading for seven seconds.

The researchers at Post 1, although they saw nothing, found that all their instruments were agitated and they began shooting pictures with color infrared film. When developed the film clearly showed the light their comrades observed, though they had never seen it.

"The fact that one group could view the light, while another directly down the tracks could not, could also have a scientific explanation," Frizzell said. "A refraction effect could make it visible in one direction and not in the other. It happens when the refraction index changes, like the effect of making a diamond invisible by dropping it in a glass of water."

The "Hookerman" is a modern-day legend in this part of northern New Jersey. It had its origins nearly a century ago in 1885, when Samuel Crook, a train conductor for the High Bridge Railroad, lost his right arm while uncoupling two cars. Crook's arm was replaced with an artificial limb with a hook hand, so the story goes. Later, he was killed in another train accident and his ghost is said to wander the tracks at night, swinging a lantern by the end of the hook, searching for his lost arm.

Robert E. Jones, now deceased, the leader of the group during that investigation, was a former high-school teacher of biology, physics, chemistry and mathematics who had done graduate work in science at St. John's University. In the 1960s, he worked for Grumman Aerospace as an engineer for NASA's manned lunar module project, and later was a systems analyst for the Defense Department's anti-ballistic missile system.

"There's no denying It exists now, because we have the photographic proof," said Jones. Jones became involved in investigating the mystery light in the Garden State in 1972, when he happened to hear about it at a party.

According to Vestigian Bill Wagner, an electronics engineer who has studied reports of such lights from all over the country, there are about 90 different lights, half of them commonly are attributed to ghosts, including 20 that appear over railroad tracks or roads covering old rail beds.

Jones, Wagner and the other Vestigians have all but eliminated ghosts as a possible cause for the New Jersey light. Spectral apparitions, they say, do not produce electrical and radioactive readings.

"An analysis of the photographs we took that night indicated we didn't have a ghost there," Jones said. "We had what looked like and acted like an energy field, one that fluctuated in size and intensity."

In a check with seismologists at the Lamont-Doherty Geological Observatory in Palisades, New York, it was discovered that a mild tremor shook Long Valley only 13 days after the spook light was photographed on November 20, 1976. An earthquake recording device placed atop Schooley's Mountain later showed that five additional quakes, small but clearly detectable, occurred in the region over the next six months.

Jones believed the metal rails acted as huge antennae, accumulating subsurface current, which built up and was finally discharged into the atmosphere. The discharge ionizes or electrically charges the air over the tracks, yielding a kind of glow that is visible when seen from a distance. Thus, the mystery light is not caused by some trainman's ghost swinging a lantern, Jones claimed, but by spurts of electrical discharge caused by pressures beneath the earth's surface.

But of course, there are the alleged sightings of the "Hookerman." A 25-year-old Long Valley resident claims to have seen the "Hookerman" walking down the tracks early one morning some years ago. He described him as "an old man in his 60s or 70s, dressed in tattered overalls with suspenders. He had a gray beard and was carrying something at his side, but when I yelled to him, he just kept walking down the tracks, away from me. I didn't know at the time who he was, or I'd have followed him."

Newark:
(Directions: eastern New Jersey along New Jersey Turnpike)
Multiple moving lights have appeared to watchers in Washington Township near Newark.
(Source: Atlas of the Mysterious in North America by Rosemary Ellen Guiley)

Jersey City:
(Directions: eastern New Jersey along I-70)
Strange lights in the belfry of St. Joseph's Catholic Church, which have illuminated two round windows near the base of the steeple, were first observed in 1924. They would always fade and reappear in ten to twenty minutes and appear to change their color from white to amber to pink to yellow. They are inactive now.

Reporters from the *Jersey City Journal* apparently proved that the lights were not reflections. Photographs revealed that the lights were as clear and bright as lighted windows in the lower part of the church. Moreover, they were seen as late as 9 a.m. when street and other night lights had been extinguished.

This episode has a sad note. Matthew Guarino, the 64-year-old sexton, announced one night that he was going to climb into the belfry in an effort to solve the mystery. Searchers found him dead in a seat in the choir loft from a heart attack.

NEW MEXICO

Llano:
(Directions: just NW of Taos on Hwy 3)
Multiple moving lights have been seen along a river near the town. Near the Sangre de Cristo Mountains just northwest of Taos, on Highway 3, some

claim to see lights glowing over the Arroyo Honda. First seen in July 1966 these 'bouncing' lights were accompanied by flying rocks and were bluish or grayish.

NEW YORK

Hudson Valley:
(Directions: Hudson Corridor begins NE of NYC & runs into western CT; US Hwy 9 & 9W runs through center of NYC, while I-84 cuts through the area in western CT)

This area north of New York City has been famous for years for its breathtaking scenery and its spooky stories and sightings. Early Dutch settlers heard the ghostly ninepins that seduced Rip Van Winkle, and this same valley is where Ichabod Crane met the headless horseman. Ghost lights appear throughout the valley.

(Source: Atlas of the Mysterious in North America by Rosemary Ellen Guiley)

NORTH CAROLINA

Big Laurel:
There have been reports of two to three moving lights seen near here.

(Source: Atlas of the Mysterious in North America by Rosemary Ellen Guiley)

Blowing Rock:
(Directions: near Pisgah National Forest on US Hwy 321 and Rt. 181)

On August 24, 1988, Dr. Donald Anderson and his wife, Hermine, saw what seemed like a command performance of the Rocky Knob phenomenon described later. For hours, the Andersons saw lateral flashes of orange-pinkish light, again resembling fireworks. No sound was heard to accompany the light show.

(Source: Atlas of the Mysterious in North America by Rosemary Ellen Guiley)

Brown Mountain:

(Directions: Hwy 181 between Morganton & Lenoir)

Brown Mountain

These mysterious lights are by far the most famous lights in this region. These lights appear over Brown Mountain, a low tree-covered summit near Linville, North Carolina. Local residents and service station operators will gladly direct visitors to Wiseman's View, where the best views of the lights are consistently obtained. There are other good observation points, and these are often identified by roadside advertisements. These lights are seen most often, due to Linville's close proximity to the Great Smokey Mountains National Park.

The lights usually appear during fair weather, although they have been seen through mist so heavy that the mountain itself was lost. They resemble toy balloons, often pinkish or red in color, rising up from the mountains, hovering for a few minutes, then vanishing into the darkness. Old-timers from the Linville area remember occasions when the sky was so filled with the lights that "....the night looked like it was on fire..."

Brown Mountain's mysterious globes are extremely shy and when approached, they simply vanish into thin air. Attempts to climb the mountain (which is quite dangerous, as the area around Linville is still wild) and get near the light often fail. However, an observation tower was built on Brown Mountain in the early 1960s. One night, a globe raced toward a group of observers and passed within inches of them. Unfortunately, this close brush did not yield any new data, but the occupants of the observation tower received severe headaches for their experience and some speculated that the light was an effect of nuclear radiation, as some of the observers in the lonely tower seemed to have symptoms of radiation sickness!

This analysis, like all others, fell short of explaining the mystery because there is no evidence of radioactive material in the vicinity of Brown Mountain. Attempts to explain the lights as refraction of street lamps from nearby towns fell through when it was pointed out that the light had been observed by early

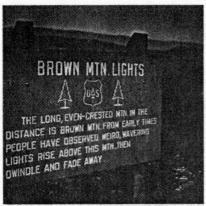

One of the signs directing visitors to the elusive Brown Mountain Lights

explorers and was often mentioned in Indian lore.

There have been attempts to determine the origin of the Brown Mountain lights. The first such investigation was made by the Smithsonian Institution in 1919. After extensive research, the report suggested that the lights could possibly be similar in nature to the Andes Lights of South America. The Andes Lights are large discharges of static electricity, but they only occur in the Andes at altitudes of 15,000 feet or more, and furthermore they do not occur in the air like the Brown Mountain lights. The Smithsonian, in effect, was stumped by the lights.

In 1922, the U.S. Geological Survey also sent an expedition to solve the mystery of the lights. The expedition's report stated that 47% of the lights were caused by reflections of automobile headlights, and the balance were due to various factors such as brush fires and will-o'-the-wisps. The local mountain lore laughed at this explanation saying that there weren't enough roads around the area to reflect that many lights. Anyway, the people said, the lights continued to appear after the Great Flood of 1916 washed out all roads and cut off electric service throughout the entire area. Historians at the University of North Carolina ridiculed the report even further by pointing out the Cherokee legends dating back to 1200 mention the lights and that the German engineer, Gerard William de Brahm, was the first one to write about the lights in 1771. The "headlight reflection" theory was promptly forgotten thereafter.

The report by George Rogers Mansfield in its entirety follows:

"For many years 'mysterious lights' have been seen near Brown Mountain, in the northern part of Burke County, N.C., about 12 miles northwest of Morganton. Some have thought that these lights were of supernatural origin; others have dreamed that they might indicate enormous mineral deposits; and have looked upon them as a natural wonder that lent interest to all vacation trips to the region.

"In October, 1913, at the urgent request of Representative E.Y. Webb, of North Carolina, a member of the United States Geological Survey, D.B.

Sterrett, was sent to Brown Mountain to observe these lights and to determine their origin. After a few days investigation Mr. Sterrett declared that the lights were nothing but locomotive headlights seen over the mountain from the neighboring heights. This explanation was too simple and prosaic to please anyone who was looking for some supernatural or unusual cause of the lights, and when they were seen after the great flood of 1916, while no trains were running in the vicinity, even some of those who had accepted Mr. Sterrett's explanation felt compelled to abandon it.

"As time went on, the interest in the lights became more general, and as one after another local investigator failed to discover their origin, the mystery seemed to grow deeper. Finally Senators Simmons and Overman prevailed upon the Geological Survey to make a second and more thorough investigation of these puzzling lights. The present writer, to whom the task of making this investigation was assigned, spent two weeks near Brown Mountain in March and April, 1922, and took observations on seven evenings, on four of them until after midnight, from hillsides that afforded favorable views of the lights. The results of the work are reported here.

"The writer gratefully acknowledges his indebtedness to Messrs. R.T. Claywell, A.M. and Charles Kistler, and H.L. Millner, of Morganton, who gave him much information and assisted him in many ways in his investigation. Joseph Loven, of Cold Springs, and H.C. Martin, of Lenoir, accompanied him on some of the evenings of observation. G.E. Moore, of Lenoir, furnished valuable information. F.H. May, of Lenoir, organized a party to accompany him to the summit of Brown Mountain and generously rendered much valuable aid. Monroe Coffey and Theodore Crump, of the United States Forest Service, extended to him the hospitality of their camp on Brown Mountain and joined in the investigation.

"Drs. W.J. Humphreys, Herbert Lyman and Mr. C.F. Talman, of the United States Weather Bureau, obligingly furnished correspondence and unpublished manuscript relating to the Brown Mountain light, and W.W. Scott, of Washington, kindly lent a scrapbook containing copies of his own and other published articles relating to Brown Mountain.

"The writer is also indebted to his colleagues of the Geological Survey for helpful suggestions and discussions, particularly to Arthus Keith for information about the geology of Brown Mountain region and to R.H. Sargent, J.B. Mertie, Jr., and A.C. Spencer for aid in the interpretation of instrumental observations.

"The shape and general elevation of Brown Mountain are shown on the accompanying map. Its eastern ridge forms part of the boundary between Burke and Caldwell counties. Its top is plateau-like and reaches a maximum elevation of about 2,600 feet. It is partly cut away by southward lowing branches of Johns river and is separated from more intricately carved uplands on the northwest, north and northeast by Upper and Wilson creeks and their tributaries. Seen from a distance from almost any direction Brown Mountain appears as a ridge having a nearly even sky line.

"The geologic features of the Brown Mountain region are the southward extension of the features seen farther north, which are described and mapped in the Cranberry folio No. 90 of the series of folios of the Geologic Atlas of the United States. There is nothing unique or unusual in the geology of Brown Mountain. Most of the mountain is composed of the Cranberry granite, a rock which also underlies many square miles on the north side of the Blue Ridge.

"The Caldwell Power Co. has drilled a series of holes, 50 to nearly 100 feet deep, along the lower part of the east slope of Brown Mountain preliminary to the location of a tunnel. Through the kindness of H.L. Millner, an officer of the company, the writer was permitted to examine the ores taken from these holes. Most of them consisted of ordinary granite, though a few included masses of rock of other kinds. The man who surveyed the line for the tunnel reported local magnetic attraction amounting to a deflection of about 6 degrees, but though representative pieces of all the different kinds of cores were presented to the compass needle they produced no noticeable effect. Dip-needle tests made to determine magnetic conditions at Brown Mountain gave readings of 41 ½ degrees which is slightly greater than those made at Loven's or at Gingercake Mountain (40 degrees) but less than those made at Blowing Rock (43 degrees) and at the Perkins place, near Adako, (45 degrees).

"So far as the writer is aware the first published account of the light was given in a dispatch from Linville Falls to the Charlotte Daily Observer, dated September 23, 1913, in which its discovery is credited to members of the Morganton Fishing Club, who saw it 'more than two years ago' but who were 'laughed at and accused of seeing things at night.' This account is quoted in part below:

"'The mysterious light that is seen just above the horizon almost every night from Rattlesnake Knob, near Cold Springs, on the Morganton Road....is still baffling all investigators....With punctual regularity the light rises in a southeasterly direction from the point of observation just over the lower slope of Brown Mountain, first about 7:30 p.m. and again at 10 o'clock. It looks much like a toy fire balloon, a distinct ball, with no atmosphere about it....It is much smaller than the full moon, much larger than any star and very red. It rises in the far distance from beyond Brown Mountain, which is about 6 miles from Rattlesnake Knob, and after going up a short distance, wavers and goes out in less than one minute....It does not always appear in exactly the same place, but varies what must amount in the distance to several miles. The light is visible at all seasons, so Mr. Anderson Loven, an old and reliable resident testifies....There seems to be no doubt that the light rises from some point in the wide, level country between Brown Mountain and the South Mountains, a distance of about 12 miles, though it is possible that it rises at a still greater distance.'

"In this article to the Charlotte Daily Observer the discovery of the lights is assigned to a date 'more than two years ago', but conversation with B.S. Gaither, of Morganton, who participated in the fishing party mentioned, and who was the one who first saw the lights, elicited the fact that they were observed in 1908 or 1909. Rev. C.E. Gregory, who in 1910 built a cottage on the little knoll near Loven's hotel at Cold Springs, presumably the Rattlesnake Knob referred to, was, according to local oral reports, the first to give much attention to the lights and bring them to public notice.

"H.L. Millner, an engineer living at Morganton, states that he did railroad surveying all through the mountains north of Brown Mountain in 1897, 1899 to 1903, and in 1905. He afterward spent many summer vacations in those mountains but says that he never saw the lights and never heard of them until 1910. Similar testimony is given by the Rev. Albert Sherrill, who served two churches in the country around Brown Mountain. In a letter to Dr. W.J. Humphrey dated January 25, 1922, he says:

"'For four years I traveled the roads to these churches and visited in the homes of the people all about this mountain. I held revival services day and night, which gave me the chance of observation at night. This was from 1909 to 1912, inclusive. At no time in all these years did I SEE a light or HEAR OF one....Two years after I left there was the first I ever heard of it.'

"On the other hand, Col. Wade H. Harris, editor of the Charlotte Daily Observer, from which the first description of the light, quoted above, was taken, states in a letter dated October 2, 1921, addressed to Senator Simmons, that 'there is a record that it (the light) has puzzled the people since and before the days of the Civil War.' R.T. Claywell, of Morganton, says that people used to come to Burke county 60 years ago to see the lights. Joseph Loven, of Cold Springs, says that he noticed the lights as early as 1897, when he moved to his present home by Loven's hotel, but that he had heard nothing about them and paid no attention to them until Mr. Gregory came, in 1910.

"In October, 1913, Mr. Strerren, of the United States Geological Survey made his investigation as a result of which he decided that the lights were locomotive headlights. He did not visit Rattlesnake Knob but went unaccompanied to Brown Mountain, where he made his observations.

"A newspaper article on the lights, by W.W. Scott, published November 10, 1915, aroused much local interest and started newspaper discussions as a result of which several expeditions, made up of local observers, visited Brown Mountain early in the winter of 1915 and in the spring of 1916 and attempted to determine the character and source of the lights. The members of these expeditions made some interesting observations but did not satisfactorily achieve their object.

"Mr. H.C. Martin, of Lenoir, states that on April 11, 1916, he and Dr. L.H. Coffey organized an expedition to study the Brown Mountain light. Each party subdivided into several groups and signals were arranged that whichever group first saw the light should fire a pistol. Doctor Coffey's party saw the light over the summit of Adams Mountain at 8:10 and again at 9:45, over a point somewhat farther south. About 5:10 a.m. they saw the light again over the south end of Adams Mountain. None of these appearances was seen by Mr. Martin's party, but about 11:52 his party saw two lights (floating globes), 'apparently about the size of ordinary street lights of Lenoir seen from the distance of about 1 mile,' flash out among the trees on the east side of Brown Mountain about one-eighth of the distance down from the summit. These lights moved horizontally southeastward, floating in and out of the ravines, along the mountain side past a dead pine tree in Mr. Martin's line of sight for a distance, again passing the line of the dead tree. At 12:13 the lights disappeared as suddenly as they came. These lights were not seen by Dr. Coffey's party.

"In the summer of 1916 a great flood swept down the valley of Catawba river washing out bridges and railroad tracks and suspending all railroad traffic in and about Morganton, so that for several weeks no trains came within 40 to 50 miles of Rattlesnake Knob, yet during that period the lights were reported to be seen as usual. This fact showed that the Brown Mountain lights could not be ascribed solely to locomotive headlights.

"Late in 1919 the question of the origin of the Brown Mountain light was brought to the attention of the Smithsonian Institution and referred to the United States Weather Bureau. Descriptions given in letters from trustworthy observers led Dr. W.J. Humphreys, of that Bureau, to decide that the light was an electrical discharge analogous to the Andes light of South America. The Andes light and its possible relation to the Brown Mountain light became the subject of a paper presented by Dr. Herbert Lyman before a meeting of the American Meteorological Society held at the Weather Bureau in Washington in April, 1921. Soon thereafter the suggestions of the physicists of the Weather Bureau were embodied in a bulletin on the Brown Mountain light issued by the National Geographic Society, in which this light was represented as manifestation of the Andes light. Neither the Weather Bureau nor the National Geographic Society, however, had sent an investigator to Brown Mountain to observe the lights.

"Those who have seen the lights from the south or east may with justice contend that no locomotive headlights can be seen to the north or northwest. A good topographic map, however, shows many roads on which an automobile headlight might intervene between an observer and Brown Mountain in such a way as to give much the same effect that one would get in viewing it over the mountain from Loven's or Blowing Rock.

"There are two buildings on the summit of Brown Mountain. One of these is owned by the Brown Mountain club and the other is a forest service station. Lights in these and the fires of campers are the only lights known to originate on Brown Mountain and are the only lights that have been seen on the mountain by observers on the mountain. There are also some buildings on the southern spurs of Brown and Adams mountains. Seen from favorable viewpoints these might furnish lights that could be interpreted as manifestations of the Brown Mountain light.

"For some years there have been lumber camps in Upper creek west of Brown Mountain. Some of the buildings at these camps are on the sides of the valley or on Ripshin Ridge. Viewed from favorable positions lights in these buildings might be ascribed to the Brown Mountain light.

"Rare electrical discharges similar to those reported from western Virginia may take place on Brown Mountain or on other ridges on the Blue Ridge front, but they could have nothing in common with the ordinary Brown Mountain light either in appearance or in regularity of occurrence.

"The lights seen by Mr. Martin from Adams Mountain can probably not be satisfactorily explained after so long a lapse in time. There is no reason to attribute to them super-natural or unusual origin and they can not be explained as due to Mirage, which is Mr. Martin's idea. The suggestion that they might have been caused by moonshiners carrying lanterns has been rejected because of the roughness of the east side of Brown Mountain and because the distance that the lights seemed to travel in 20 minutes. They might be due to fireflies flying relatively near Mr. Martin yet appearing unduly large because his eyes were focused on the distant hillside, the appearance of going in and out of ravines being due to intermittence in the lights, but H.S. Barber, an entomologist of the Division of Insects of the National Museum, to whom the matter was referred states that this explanation though possible, is improbable, chiefly because of the lateness of *the hour of observation.*

"In the article published in the Charlotte Daily Observer *in September, 1913, it was stated that the lights were first observed from a place near Loven's hotel, at Cold Springs, and as late as November, 1915. Mr. Scott, in his newspaper article cited above, stated that 'Mr. Loven's is the only place from which has been seen the mysterious light that rises over Brown Mountain.' By the spring of 1916, however, the lights were being observed from several places near Lenoir. More recently they were seen from Blowing Rock, which is visited by many tourists, who find accommodations at several flourishing hotels. The lights furnish one of the many attractions afforded by this remarkably well situated and delightful little town. Among the other localities from which the Brown Mountain lights are said to have been seen are the slopes of Gingercake Mountain about a mile and a half southwest of Cold Spring, and the toll gate on the Yonahlossee road, on the south slope of Grandfather Mountain. It is also reported that they have been seen from Morganton and from other points in the valley southeast of Brown Mountain.*

"It is significant that, though many persons have from time to time camped on Brown Mountain and have spent nights watching for the lights, yet, so far as the writer has been able to ascertain, NO ONE HAS ACTUALLY OBSERVED THE LIGHT ON BROWN MOUNTAIN WHEN HE HIMSELF WAS ON THAT MOUNTAIN, but, as in Doctor Coffey's observation, it has been seen from Brown Mountain as apparently over Adams Mountain or some hills farther south. Monroe Coffey and Theodore Crump, of the United States Forest Service, have spent many nights in and about Brown Mountain and have built a fire-control station on the summit of the mountain near the cabin of the Brown Mountain club, but at the time of the writer's visit neither of them had ever seen the Brown Mountain light.

"In his letter to Senator Simmons already cited Colonel Harris writes as follows concerning the light:

"'It is a pale white light, as one seen through a ground glass globe, and there is a faint irregularity shaped halo around it. It is confined to a prescribed circle, appearing three or four times in quick succession, then disappearing for 20 minutes or half an hour, when it repeats within the same circle.'

"Prof. W.G. Perry, of the Georgia School of Technology, in a letter dated December 15, 1919, addressed to Dr. C.G. Abbot, of the Smithsonian Institution, described the light as seen from the Cold Spring locality as follows:

"'We occupied a position on a high ridge. Across several intervening ridges rose Brown Mountain, some 8 miles away. After sunset we began to

watch the Brown Mountain direction. Suddenly there blazed in the sky, apparently above the mountain, near one end of it, a steadily glowing ball of light. It appeared to be about 10 degrees above the upper line of the mountain, blazed with a slightly yellow light, lasted about half a minute, and then abruptly disappeared. It was not alike the star from a bursting rocket or Roman candle, though brighter.

"'We were impressed with the following facts: The region about Brown Mountain and between our location and the mountain is a wild, practically uninhabited region - a confusion of mountain peaks, ridges and valleys. Viewing the lights from a fixed position our estimate of their location was most inexact; the varying color (almost white, yellowish, reddish) may have been due to mist in the atmosphere; the view of the lights was a direct one and not a reflection; there seemed to be no regularity in their time or appearance; they came suddenly into being blazed steadily, and as suddenly disappeared; they appeared against the sky and not against the side of the mountain.

"'Others who have seen this phenomenon make very different reports of their observation; and some who have seen it several times report that they have seen it in varying fashion; sometimes the light appears stationary (as was uniformly the case when I saw it); sometimes, it appears to move rapidly, upward, downward, horizontally.'

"Rev. C.E. Gregory is reported to have noted upon one occasion that the light appeared like a ball of incandescent gas in which a seething motion could be observed.

"Many explanations of the Brown Mountain lights have been offered. The principal ones that have come to the notice of the writer are briefly outlined below.

"1. Will-o'-the-wisp. A light called will-o'-the-wisp is sometimes seen over marshy places and is supposed to be due to spontaneous combustion of marsh gas. There are, however, no marshy places on or about Brown Mountain, and the lights seen by the writer could not be ascribed to such a cause.

"2. Phosphorus. It has been suggested that the lights may be caused in some way by the element phosphorus. Phosphorus, however, is so easily oxidized that it does not occur in the free state. It is usually locked up in stable and relatively insoluble chemical compounds and therefore can not be a cause of the Brown Mountain light.

"3. Phosphorescence (fox fire). Some organic bodies, such as stumps or logs, become luminous or phosphorescent by slow oxidization and combustion in the course of their decay. Such lights are too feeble to be seen at a distance of several miles and are unlike the lights seen by the writer.

"4. Radium emanations. The late F.H. Hossfeld is reported to have found a piece of pitchblende, an ore or radium, near the southwest end of Brown Mountain, and some therefore think that Brown Mountain may contain a large body of radium ore, which might by emanation produce the observed lights. So far as the writer has been able to learn the material that was found is not accurately known. The specimen itself has been lost; but pitchblende, even if it occurred in large deposits, could not give rise to lights like those seen over Brown Mountain. No known radium ore shows that kind of luminosity.

"5. Chemical reaction between hydrogen sulphide and lead oxide. In a letter received from Mr. E.C. Ivey of Hickory, it is suggested that the lights may be so caused, and it is stated that both hydrogen sulphide and lead oxide occur in Brown Mountain and that hydrogen sulphide will ignite in the presence of lead oxide. Sulphur springs occur on the west side of Brown Mountain and lead prospects are reported on the east side, but the possibility that there is any direct relation between them is so slight as to be highly improbable.

"6. 'Blockade' (illicit) stills. Many stills have been operated by 'moonshiners' in the vicinity of Brown Mountain. A man who claims to have been an eyewitness states that screens are placed about these stills to shut off the light from the fires but that from time to time the fires are raked out and the covers of the stills removed, so that the clouds of steam which arise from them are illuminated by the fires below. The 'moonshiners' are also said to use lights for signaling. It is possible that the light with 'seething motion' seen by Mr. Gregory may have been of this origin, but there are not enough such stills and they probably would not be in sufficiently continuous operation to produce lights in the number and in the regularity of appearance of those seen at Brown Mountain.

"7. St. Elmo's fire. St. Elmo's fire is a brushlike, luminous, electrical discharge that sometimes takes place from masts, lightning, conductors, and other pointed objects, especially during thunderstorms. In his correspondence with Messrs. Clark and Perry, the trustworthy observers already mentioned, Dr. C.G. Abbot of the Smithsonian Institution, suggested that the Brown Mountain light may be due to St. Elmo's fire, but there seems to be little in common between the lights seen by the writer and St. Elmo's fire as usually described. In a second letter to Doctor Abbot, dated January 9, 1920, Professor Perry states the cause clearly when he says, 'My own impression of St. Elmo's fire and similar phenomena was that it occurred at the extremity of some solid conductor instead of occurring, as in the case of the Brown Mountain lights, in the air, at a great distance from any object.'

"8. Andes light. The name Andes light, according to information furnished to the writer by Dr. Herbert Lyman, of the United States Weather Bureau, is given to a very striking luminous discharge of electricity seen over the crest of the Andes in Chile, where ordinary thunderstorms are almost unknown. The mountain peaks appear to act as gigantic, lightning rods, between which and the clouds SILENT discharges take place on a vast scale.

"The principal writer on the Andes light is Dr. Walter Knoche, who was for several years director of the Central Meteorological and Geophysical Institute at Santiago, Chile, and who says that he has seen this light at distances greater than 300 miles. Most of the discharges appear to produce glimmering lights that have circular borders. The flashes are bright at their starting points but diminish rapidly in intensity and then slowly disappear. The area of this silent discharge is at first small and lies over the main cordillera, but it soon extends far over the zenith and sometimes reaches over the coast cordillera and out to sea. The phenomenon is best seen in a clear sky.

"Dr. Guy Hinsdale, in the Scientific Monthly for September, 1919, reports that in Western Virginia, where there are 'numerous parallel ridges with intervening deep and narrow valleys, it occasionally happens that an electric discharge takes place from the summits of these ridges into the atmosphere. There is nothing audible, but merely the sudden glow of the higher clouds in the dark night.'

"9. Mirage. Mr. H.C. Martin, in the Lenoir Topic for April 19, 1916, and afterward in conversation with the writer, has suggested that the lights may be due to mirage. He thinks that air currents of different temperature and density may produce between them reflecting surfaces, from which bright stars or other lights might be reflected in such way as to produce the effects commonly seen. According to this explanation the wavering of the reflecting surface would cause the sudden appearance, wavering, and disappearance of the light.

"A mirage is a phenomenon of the daytime rather than of the night. The requisite conditions are that the air must be still and that the lower layers, heated by radiation from the underlying surface, must become less dense than the overlying layers and yet be unable to escape. With the least disturbance of these unstable conditions the overheated air suddenly 'spills' upward and the mirage disappears. The conditions in a mountain gorge such as that of Wilson creek east of Brown Mountain are entirely unfavorable to mirage, for as soon as the lower air becomes warmed it may escape from the neighboring uplands. Yet Mr. Martin, in seeking in air currents of different temperature and density an explanation of the light, has hit upon what the writer believes to be a fundamental element of the problem, as will be more fully explained below.

"10. Locomotive headlights. D.B. Sterrett, of the United States Geological Survey, who investigated the light on October 11, 1913, noted that the headlights of westbound Southern Railway locomotives could be observed from Brown Mountain and that they were brilliant enough to be seen in the same straight line from Loven's place, 6 miles beyond. He checked up the train schedules and concluded that headlights were 'beyond doubt' the cause of the Brown Mountain light. Objection to this view has been raised on the ground that a locomotive headlight casts a beam, which, like that of a searchlight as frequently seen, can be readily identified. This objection is considered under the heading 'Conclusions.'

"11. Automobile headlights. Powerful headlights on automobiles have been suggested as a source of the Brown Mountain light. The objection made to this suggestion is similar to that made to the suggestion they are caused by locomotive headlights, and it fails for the same reasons. When seen at long distance the two kinds of headlights behave in a similar manner. Of the 23 lights recorded by instrumental observation in the investigation here reported, 11 were probably automobile headlights.

"The investigation in 1922. Methods employed. After a conference in Morganton with men who are familiar with the lights the writer set out to take observations at the place near Loven's hotel and at other places from which, according to reports, the lights could be seen, Brown Mountain itself being one of the places. The instruments used consisted of a 15-inch plane table (a square board, mounted on three legs), a telescopic alidade, pocket and dip-needle compasses, a barometer for measuring elevations, a field glass, a flash light, and a camera, besides topographic maps of the region.

"In making the observations a topographic map was fastened flat on the board, which was leveled and the map turned to a position in which the directions north, south, east and west on the map corresponded with the same direction on the ground. Sights were then taken to known landmarks with the alidade, which is essentially a ruler fitted with a sighting telescope, and corresponding lines were drawn along the ruler of the map. The meeting-point of the lines thus drawn marked the location of the observer's instrument on the map. From this location, which was determined in the daytime, sights were taken at night with the alidade on the different lights seen, and lines of direction to them were drawn on the map. The telescope on the alidade swings in a vertical as well as a horizontal plane and can therefore be used for measuring vertical angles along the lines of sight. The dip-needle compass is so arranged that the needle swings in a vertical instead of in a horizontal plane. It is used to detect differences in magnetic attraction.

"Three stations were occupied - one on the knoll by the cottage formerly occupied by Rev. C.E. Gregory, near Loven's hotel; one in a field on the east slope of Gingercake Mountain; and one on the terrace in front of the summer residence of Miss Cannon, at Blowing Rock. These stations are marked on the map by letters A, B, and C, respectively. Two nights were spent on Brown Mountain, but the conditions were so unfavorable that no station was occupied there. At each station at which observations were made vertical angles to parts of Brown Mountain were noted, dip-needles readings were made and photographs were taken. Vertical angles were also measured when practicable from each station to each light seen. The procedure adopted was first to get a line of sight to the light and then to note its time of appearance and measure its vertical angle, but occasionally a light remained visible for so short a time that it had disappeared before the telescope could be trained upon it and a line drawn to fix its direction. Few records were kept of lights for which lines of direction were not drawn, but the total number seen may have been nearly twice the number recorded. The atmosphere proved too hazy for satisfactory photographs.

"The train registers at Connelly Springs and at Hickory were examined, and subsequently train schedules for the evenings of observations were obtained from many station agents throughout the region.

"The observations obtained in the field were afterward adjusted on the map. Many profiles along lines of sight were constructed, the vertical angles were platted, and corrections for the curvature of the earth's surface and for refraction were made. In this way the sources of some of the lights were approximately determined.

"Space does not permit a detailed statement of the individual observations made and of the inferences drawn from them. The geographic positions of the sources of light as determined by instrumental observations are only approximate because of the difficulties attending the use of the instruments in darkness. The stations were from 1,000 to 1,500 feet higher than the summit of Brown Mountain, so that the lines of sight to the lights seen all passed several hundred feet above the top of the mountain.... This fact caused the lights to appear over the mountain rather than on or below its crest, a feature noted both in the first published description of the lights, in the Charlotte Observer, and in Professor Perry's description, already quoted. The appearance of the lights as described in these two accounts, especially in that given by Professor Perry, agrees so closely with their appearance as observed by the writer that no additional description of them need be given here.

"At Station A (elevation 3,550 feet), near Loven's hotel, which is the place from which the light was first seen, the outlook is restricted on the south by a projecting ridge which cuts off the view of the region west of the eastern part of Morganton approximately the region southwest of line 3 on the map, northward from Lenoir the county becomes rougher, and few lights from areas north of that place may be seen from Loven's, so that practically all lights that originate beyond Brown Mountain as seen from Station A lie in an arc between Lenoir and line 3 and are therefore seen over Brown Mountain. This fact accounts for the original association of the observed lights with Brown Mountain and hence for the name 'Brown Mountain light.' It also probably accounts for the 'prescribed circle' of appearances of the light noted in Colonel Harris' letter to Senator Simmons.

"On the evening of March 29 the writer was accompanied to Station A by Joseph, Robert and Earl Loven, of Cold Springs, and Robert Ward, of Morganton. The light on line 1, when viewed in the telescope of the alidade, was accompanied by one or two subordinate lights. Its position was unchanged throughout the evening, but it varied in brightness. At some times, for long periods, it was so dim that it was practically invisible to the naked eye, though it was faintly shown in the telescope. At other times it flared brightly, so that Joseph Loven pronounced it a true manifestation of the Brown Mountain light. Its position and its relation to the accompanying lights were not affected by the flaring. Two of the observers said that they could see it waver or move, but as seen through the telescope each time this statement was made its position was found to be unchanged.

"At about 8:40 lights appeared successively and nearly in the same line over the middle of the mountain. The directions of these lights are shown in lines 2a and 2b. Line 2a is tangent to a curve in the track of the Southern Railway about a mile and a half northwest of Conover. From train schedules it was determined that a westbound freight train passed this curve at the time noted. Line 2b is probably a poorer sight at the same light and may represent an error of observation due the writer's inability in the darkness to use the cross hairs of the instrument. It may, however, point to an automobile headlight.

"Lines 3 and 4 are credited to automobiles. Line 5 represents a locomotive headlight near Connelly Springs.

"The flares seen from Station A all looked much alike and corresponded closely with the description quoted from Professor Perry's letter, Robert Loven said that the lights as he had usually seen them were so much brighter than these that he did not think the party had actually seen the Brown

Mountain light. Joseph Loven, however, said that he had seen the lights both when they were brighter and when they were not so bright, and he was satisfied that the lights observed were a fair average of the Brown Mountain light.

"Station B, on Gingercake Mountain, is about 500 feet higher than Station A, and the arc over which the lights are visible is correspondingly increased. Brown Mountain covers about half of this arc. The fellow observers at Station B were Joseph Loven and Robert Ward. On the evening of April 1 the mist in the valley was so dense that only one observation could be made - the one on line 6, which is ascribed to an automobile on the State highway near Drexel. The highway runs for some distance nearly parallel with the railroad.

"The conditions for observation on the night of April 2, though poor, were more favorable than on the preceding night, and sights 7 to 16, inclusive, were recorded on the corresponding lines. At 7:45 and 8:55 lights flared out over the south end of Brown Mountain on lines 8 and 12, respectively. When corrected these observations fell on the same line, near the station Drexel. A report from the station agent shows that westbound freight trains on the Southern Railway left Drexel at the times specified. Lights 9, 10, 11, 14, and 15 are ascribed to automobiles.

"Throughout the evening a light, one of a small group, was seen on line 13. Its position remained the same, but it flared at longer or shorter intervals. Between flares it could be dimly seen with the naked eye. As corrected, the position of this source of light seemed to fall near the dam at the foot of the big reservoir on Linville river, not shown on the map.

"Train No. 35, a westbound passenger train on the Southern Railway, is due at Connelly Springs at 12:35 a.m. The writer decided to remain on watch until the time for that train in order to get answers to two questions: First, could the headlight at Connelly Springs be seen from the Gingercake Mountain station over Brown Mountain and, second, if the headlight could be seen would it look like the true Brown Mountain light? Accordingly, about 10 minutes before train time the telescopic alidade was directed toward the curved track about a mile east of Connelly Springs. All observers then waited for the train. At 12:33 a light flared over Brown Mountain and was seen in the telescope on line 16. Though the train was 8 minutes behind its schedule all observers were convinced that the light seen was the headlight of train No. 35. To the writer it looked much like the other lights that Mr. Loven had called the Brown Mountain light on this and on preceding evenings. Mr. Loven himself declared that it looked like the Brown Mountain light, though he thought it had a slightly more bluish tint. Upon later examination of the train register at Connelly Springs it was found that train No. 35 had arrived at the station at 12:35. Allowing for the time required for the train to run from the curve to the station at Connelly Springs the train register may be confidently regarded as verifying the observation.

"On this night, as on the first night, all the lights seen looked much alike, though some of the flares were brighter than others. Mr. Loven was asked several times if he felt satisfied that the lights seen by the party were actually the Brown Mountain light. He replied that he was satisfied and that it was a fair average exhibition.

"On April 3 Station C was established at Blowing Rock, at an elevation of about 3,700 feet. Although not so high as the station on Gingercake Mountain this station commands a wide, sweeping view of the country to the south, a view through nearly a quarter of a circle, but Brown Mountain occupies only a small part of this space. The moon was shining brightly, but a heavy mist overhung the valley and completely obscured Brown Mountain. H.C. Martin, of Lenoir, was present during part of the time of observation and Robert Ward, of Morganton, during the whole time.

"A steady group of lights was dimly visible most of the evening on lines 17 and 18. These lights were reddish and were accompanied by what appeared to be smoke. These lights appeared to originate on a ridge north of Mulberry creek. Their smoky appearance suggests that they came from brush fires.

"At 8:35 a reddish light appeared on line 19. If flared twice and then, as seen by the unaided eye, apparently went out, but it continued for a time to show dimly in the telescope. The line of sight corrected for curvature and refraction clears by a short distance the mountain mass at the county line and falls near a curve of the Carolina, Clinchfield & Ohio Railway about a mile southeast of Spruce Pine. No agent is on duty at Spruce Pine at night, and thus far the writer has been unable to learn whether or not there was a southbound train on the track there at the time noted.

"Mr. Martin said that the light on line 19 looked very much like the Brown Mountain light, but that it questioned as to wherein the two differed, he replied that in the first place the light was not seen over Brown Mountain and second, it did not train off laterally or obliquely as the Brown Mountain light usually did.

"At 9:05 a light flared on line 20. The source of the light was determined to be in the streets of Lenoir. There was no northbound trains that night, so the light probably came from an automobile headlight.

"On the night of April 4, on account of unfavorable conditions, only one observation (No. 21) was obtained. This was ascribed to a locomotive headlight.

"With the exception of lights 17 and 18, ascribed to brush fires, the lights seen from Blowing Rock were practically indistinguishable in general character and appearance from those that were seen at Loven's and at Gingercake Mountain and that were said by Mr. Loven to be the Brown Mountain light. A lady at Blowing Rock declared that on a clear evening 'you could go out on the hill and see lights popping out all over the valley, all looking as much alike as so many peas in a pod.' Mr. Martin, on the other hand, said that the Brown Mountain light had distinctive features and that the party had not seen it on either evening. The principal distinctive features indicated appears to be the lateral or oblique motion above referred to.

"On April 5 the writer ascended Brown Mountain with a party organized by F.H. May of Lenoir. Theodore Crump, of the Forest Service, kindly placed at the disposal of the party his station on the summit of the mountain. Rain and fog interfered with the observations, but watch was kept from about 8 to 10:30 p.m. and again from 12:15 to 12:45 a.m. No lights were seen . On the following day, April 6, several members left the party, but Monroe Coffey of the Forest Service, joined it. That evening there was no rain, but fog prevented any extended view from the summit of the mountain. Somewhat below the summit, however, the fog was less dense, and it was possible to have seen any lights that might arise over the Brown Mountain mass. About 9:30 the party made a circuit from the summit to the hill above Parke creek, in the south-central part of the mountain, returning to the summit shortly before midnight. Had any lights arisen over the mountain some member of the party would probably have seen them, but none appeared.

"Conclusions: The writer feels confident that the lights he saw were actually a fair average display of the so-called Brown Mountain light. He not only has Mr. Loven's word to sustain this conclusion, but he is certain that the lights he saw agree closely in appearance and behavior with those originally described in the Charlotte Daily Observer and by Professor Perry.

"The lights ordinarily originate not on or near Brown Mountain but in the broad valley some miles away. This conclusion accords with original published description of the lights.

"The lights observed have nothing in common with the Andes light or with St. Elmo's fire. There is no geologic basis for the idea that the lights seen are natural wonders of any sort, but there are certain interesting surface features and atmospheric conditions that are effective in producing some of the appearances of the light.

"By reference to the man it will be noted that the Catawba Valley east of Marion is a basin-like are - an area nearly surrounded by mountains, of which the Blue Ridge on the north, with its fringe of southward-projecting spurs, is the highest and most rugged. After sunset cool air begins to creep down the tributary valleys into the basin, but the air currents come from different temperature and density. The atmospheric conditions in the basin are therefore very unstable, especially in the earlier part of the evening, before any well-defined circulatory system becomes established. At any given place in the basin the air varies in density during the evening and hence its refractiveness. The denser the air, the more it refracts light or bends waves of light emanating from any source. The humidity of the air affects its density and hence its refractive power. Mist, dust, and other fine particles tend to obscure and scatter the light refracted and to impart to it the reddish or yellowish tints so frequently observed. Thus it is that the light is most active in a clearing spell after a rain, as noted by many observers. When the mist is very dense the light is completely obscured.

"Lights that arise from any source in the basin are viewed at low angles. Even those observed from altitudes of 3,500 or 4,000 feet, the heights of the stations on Gingercake or on Blowing Rock Mountain had vertical angles of less than 3 degrees. Thus the refractive effect on the atmosphere through which the light waves must travel is at a maximum.

"The effect of variations in the density of the atmosphere between the observer and the source of the light is at one time to increase and at another time to diminish the intensity of the light. This fact accounts for the flares on lines 1 and 13. The diminution of a light after such a flare is so marked that to the casual observer or to one without a field glass the light may seem to be completely extinguished. In the telescope, however, it still appears in the same relative position, though it is somewhat fainter. Lights that are in view for brief periods, such as the headlights of automobiles or locomotives, which show only when they are turned in other directions they become extinguished so far as the observer at a given station is concerned.

"Probably few if any basins on the Blue Ridge front are so favorably located as to show as well as this one the atmospheric phenomena described, and the opportunities here for the observation of such phenomena are perhaps no less exceptional. Loven's Hotel and Blowing Rock, which are resorts that attract fishermen or tourists, are among the most favorable places of observation. The valley is fairly well settled, has a network of roads, three railroads, and several large towns, so that the possible source of light are very numerous.

"As the basin and its atmospheric conditions antedate the earliest settlement of the region it is possible that even among the first settlers some favorably situated light may have attracted attention by seeming to flare and then diminish or go out. As the country became more thickly settled the number of chance for such observations would increase. Before the advent of electric lights, however, it is doubtful whether such observations could have been sufficiently numerous to cause much comment, though some persons may have noted and remarked upon them. According to local estimates electric lights have been in use in the larger towns of the region for about 30 years. Lights from these towns viewed from the locality near Loven's, which for a long time was the only locality from which the lights were observed, are, with the exception of those from Morganton and Blowing Rock, all seen over Brown Mountain; hence the 'prescribed circle' mention by Colonel Harris.

"The use of powerful electric headlights on railway locomotives, which began about 1909, furnish new sources of strong lights in the valley and introduced an element of regularity in their appearance, which may account for the 'punctual regularity' noted in the first description. After Rev. C.E. Gregory took up his summer residence near Loven's hotel, in 1910, the Brown Mountain light began to acquire notoriety.

"Meanwhile automobiles were coming into use throughout the country, and many of them were equipped with powerful headlights. Within the last few years their number has been greatly increased, and this fact is in keeping with the general deduction already made - that on a favorable evening the lights are seen more frequently than formerly.

"During the flood of 1916, when train service was temporarily discontinued, the basin east of Marion, are disturbed, was still the scene of the intermittent flare of favorably situated lights. Automobiles were then in use in the larger towns and on some of the intervening roads, and their headlights were doubtless visible from Loven's over Brown Mountain. One need only remember the network of roads in the valley region (see topographic maps of the Morganton and Hickory quadrangles) to realize the almost infinite number of possibilities for automobile headlights to be pointed toward Brown Mountain and stations of observation beyond. It should be emphasized, too, that automobile headlights and locomotive headlights, when seen at distances and under atmospheric conditions such as those which prevail in this region, possess no characteristic that clearly distinguishes them from other lights. On the contrary, as stated by the lady at Blowing Rock, they look 'as much alike as so many peas in a pod,' though this statement should not be understood to mean that some may not be brighter than others.

"Col. Wade H. Harris, in his letter to Senator Simmons already cites, says: 'A locomotive headlight is easily and unmistakable distinguished as such not only by the rays it shoots forth but from its movement. It (the Brown

Mountain light) is as distinct in characteristics from a locomotive headlight as a candle flame is to a naked arc light.' Again, in an article in the Charlotte Observer for March 27th, 1922, the same writer adds that 'a headlight has characteristics that distinctly and unmistakably identify it as such.'

"The writer's observations, MADE IN COMPANY WITH PERSONS LONG FAMILIAR WITH THE LIGHT, failed to substantiate these statements. Of the 23 lights noted by instrumental observation recorded on lines 1 to 21, 7 proved to originate from locomotive headlights, and an eighth (No. 19) is probably of similar origin, though the data are insufficient to establish that fact but none of these 7 lights cast a beam or possessed any special quality that distinguished it from the other lights observed, and only one of them (No. 16) was known at the time of the observation to be a locomotive headlight. The other 6 were identified as such only after the lines and angles of the record had been plotted, profiles had been drawn, and train schedules had been checked up, some days after the observations were made. A locomotive headlight seen at distances such as those from which the Brown Mountain light is observed has no visible motion and emits no 'rays.' When its line of direction coincides with the line of observation the light flashes on, or if the air is misty it flares, much as an incandescent electric light flares when it is turned on. When its line of direction leaves the line of observation the light disappears just as suddenly as it came.

"The behavior of headlights in the Brown Mountain region in this respect is comparable to that of the lights of lighthouses on the Atlantic coast. From the sea wall at Glouster, Mass., the writer has repeatedly seen the light at Minots Ledge, southeast of Houston, nearly 25 miles away in a direct line. This light is identified by a series of flashes that may be represented by the numerals 1-4-3. There is not beam and there are no rays. The light can not be seen unless the air is fairly clear. Then it simply flashes once, four times, three times, and it has much the same appearance as the Brown Mountain light.

"The supposed motion of the light at times may be due to errors of observation. Reference had already been made here to the fact that two observers who were present with the writer at Station A thought they saw the light move when it was actually motionless as seen in the telescope. Some years ago McNeely DuBose, an engineer then employed near Morganton, tested observations made by himself and others by tying a cord across the fork of a tree in a place where he could see the light across the cord, and was surprised to find that the light was stationary with respect to the cord. Professor Perry, whose letter has been quoted, notes that the light was uniformly stationary when he saw it. The eye is easily deceived at night as to the stability or motion of an object, and an observer's impressions are to a considerable extent affected by his mental and physical condition at the time of observation. It is not surprising that under the circumstances different eye-witnesses give quite different accounts of the light, especially as the light may appear suddenly against a dark background with nothing nearby that can be used as a scale to determine its size or its possible motion.

"There remains the question of the identity of the Brown Mountain light as seen from Blowing Rock. Mr. Martin specified two requirements, namely, the light must be seen over lines D and F on the map. Line D is drawn to a road that seems to be thoroughfare near Brindletown. Line F is drawn tangent to the Southern Railway near Thermal City. Just east of this lie is a thoroughfare, and a short distance farther east is the tract of the Carolina, Clinchfield & Ohio Railway. Line F is drawn to the same road and railroads a few miles farther northwest.

"Automobile headlights on any of the numerous roads that point toward Blowing Rock within the area designated and south of Catawba river would be visible from Blowing Rock over Brown Mountain.

"The writer was told at Blowing Rock that a good time to see the lights was from 9:30 p.m. to 10 or a little later. The agent of the Southern Railway at Thermal City states that a northbound train on that railway passes that station at 9:30 p.m., maintaining approximately the same schedule the year round. The agent at Glenwood on the same railway reports that a train is due there at 9:53 the year round. Data for the other railroad are not available, but doubtless there are some northbound evening freight trains on it. The agreement of the train schedules with the above statement about the time to see the lights is certainly more than a coincidence.

"It may be questioned whether a locomotive headlight could be seen for a distance so great as that between Blowing Rock and Thermal City, which is about 45 miles. The Minots Ledge light, already mentioned, is rated at 75,000 candle-power by the Bureau of Lighthouses and is visible for distances greater than 25 miles. The writer was told by Mr. Chadwick, of the Engineering Department of the Southern Railway, that the headlights in common use on that system are incandescent nitrogen lamps rated at 250 watts and 32 volts. Fitted with 16-inch, silvered-copper parabolic reflectors, these lights yield about 600,000 candle-power. There is therefore no reason to doubt that the headlights would be visible at a distance of 45 miles.

"The high power of these lights accounts for the brilliancy ascribed to the Brown Mountain light by observers who have seen it when the air was exceptionally clear, and it also accounts for the fact that some of the lights *seen are brighter than others.*

"In summary it may be said that the Brown Mountain lights are clearly not of unusual nature or origin. About 47% of the lights that the writer was able to study instrumentally were due to automobile headlights, 33% to locomotive headlights, 10% to stationary lights and 10% to brush fires."

The U.S. Geological Survey, after recovering from the snafu of their first investigation, tried again a few years later. They concluded that the lights were not due to foxfire or St. Elmo's fire, and the most probable answer was spontaneous ignition of swamp gas. This "explanation" met with even greater laughter than the previous one, as everyone around Linville knew there were no swamps or marshy areas around Brown Mountain. Indeed, the U.S. Geological Survey's own maps place the nearest marshy area at about 100 miles away!

Every so often there is talk of organizing another expedition to try and unravel Brown Mountain's secrets, but all such ventures eventually fail as the would-be discoverers read of how both the Smithsonian Institution and the U.S. Geological Survey failed to uncover any plausible explanation. Meanwhile, the good folk of Linville and Morganton continue to guide tourists to viewing spots and tell their tales of the lights without wondering as to possible explanations. As J.L. Hartley, State Fire Marshal, said in 1947, "I have lived for 60 years within sight of Brown Mountain....it seems that since God made Brown Mountain, he could have made a light for it."

A researcher from Morganton believed he found the source of the fabled lights. A 47-year old search for the source of the famed "Brown Mountain Lights" may be near an end, but it appears there may be a bigger mystery to solve. Paul Rose, a Jonas Ridge nurseryman, said a dozen men stood on a tower atop Brown Mountain and watched the fabled lights flash out of nearby crevices.

"They came out in circles of about three feet in diameter," said Rose, who is leading the current expedition which hopes to solve the mystery. "The lights were in colors or red, orange and the color of the moon.

"One of the lights came to rest on the men on the tower. It gave them a static-like feeling of dizziness. When they climbed to the ground, they were unable to stand up." Rose said of the 12 men atop the 60-foot tower, 11 felt the sense of dizziness. The other felt nothing.

Rose said he believes the lights are radioactive or contain some magnetic element. "The lights seemed to come through the trees, down the mountain, under a cliff, and back up again," he said. Rose said he is anxious to get the opinion of a professional geologist, who may be able to determine why the lights would make people dizzy.

Rose and scores of volunteers carried lumber up the mountain and erected the tower so that viewers could look down into crevices from which the lights appeared to come. "I still don't know that the lights are coming from the crevice," Rose said. "But I believe we'll be able to find out."

He said hundreds of people had visited the area and seen the lights. But Rose, whose mountain nursery is located nearby said he had been viewing them for nearly 40 years.

In 1951, there was a report from a local resident of a very close encounter of this strange light. John P. Bessor, an investigator in the field, was told of a couple on the summit of Brown Mountain at around dusk when a brilliant light "as long as a man's arm" suddenly formed overhead. It emitted a sizzling noise and hovered motionless for a time, and then lengthened and shortened several times in succession.

In years past, mysterious lights in various parts of North America have sometimes been speculatively linked to Unidentified Flying Objects (UFOs). The testimony of Mr. Bessor's witnesses would however, suggest an unusual form of lightning or electrical discharge over Brown Mountain. Though lightning has received much study since the time of Benjamin Franklin it is, however, far from being completely understood. In fact, it is only comparatively recently that the existence of ball lightning has been unequivocally recognized and data collated relating to other forms of electrical discharge.

It seems reasonable, therefore, to author Malcolm Bessent, writing for the *New Horizons Research Foundation*, to suppose that the Brown Mountain lights are an untypical form of electric discharge resulting from unusual local meteorological conditions. The rock at Blowing Rock is celebrated for the strong and persistent updraft of air at that point, which suggests that the vicinity of Brown Mountain may have its own peculiarities of local climate and atmospheric circulations.

At the suggestion of the *New Horizons Research Foundation*, the writer visited Brown Mountain from September 16-18 in 1971. The weather was extremely poor, and it rained almost continuously during that time. On the first day, he reconnoitered the mountain in the hope of reaching the summit as the best place for observation. In fact, there is a small observation tower there, presumably a fire-watch post. At 6:35 p.m., while driving along a narrow track, he saw a light flash briefly above him. At that time he had no idea as to the appearance of the alleged lights, and so did not immediately realize that he had just seen one. He waited for 15 minutes and, as the light did not occur again, continued his exploration of Brown Mountain but he failed to find either a track or a footpath to the summit. As the mountain is densely wooded, and the conditions were very bad on account of the rain, he decided that the best place to make his observations would be from a hillside, perhaps one and a quarter miles from the ridge of Brown Mountain. He continued his reconnaissance until 7:30 p.m. and then left the mountain, in the hope of contacting some local informants. He did not make a watch that night, as he did not know what to expect, or what would be the best time for viewing the lights.

On the night of September 17th he maintained a watch from the chosen position on the neighboring hill from 7:30 p.m. until 1 a.m. It had rained heavily all day. The rain stopped at about 8 p.m. but the sky was heavily overcast and the air exceedingly damp and misty. However, from 8:30 p.m. until 11:00 p.m. he witnessed the lights, which showed remarkable irregularities. There were three distinct types of light that appeared consistently. Horizontally their locations varied little. Each light appeared to have its own characteristic color, frequency of occurrence and elevations. The timing was obtained by using a watch with a second hand.

Light 1 was yellowish white and appeared at intervals of 8-11 seconds, having a duration of about half a second.

Light 2 was a reddish orange in color, and appeared at intervals of 12-15 seconds, having a duration of about half a second.

Light 3 was violet in color. When it flashed the duration was only about one eighth of a second. Its occurrence was much less regular than that of the others. Sometimes there would be a series of several flashes, mutually separated by time intervals of approximately 35 seconds. These bursts would be followed by lengthy pauses with no activity until the next burst. The duration of the pauses varied between 5 minutes and 30 minutes.

According to his observations, the lights seemed to be electrical in nature, and had a distinct resemblance to lightning. However, the somewhat rhythmic cycles as described above were quite unlike what is normally expected of lightning. When he explored the next day, driving on and around the mountain, he saw that there were several homes that he judged to be approximately below the area where the lights occurred. However, without having additional observers working synchronously, it was not possible to ascertain exact spatial relationships between the houses and the lights.

While observing the phenomena he was able to take photographs of Light number 2. However, on account of the poor lighting conditions and the brief duration of the lights, and also because of characteristics of the film, it was not possible to achieve faithful color rendition of the lights. Two Nikon FTN cameras on tripod were used. One was equipped with a wide-angle lens. The film was Kodak High Speed Ektachrome 125 ASA, rated at 400 ASA. Exposure was made by trial, as a light meter was not effective in these conditions. The first ten pictures were taken at 10 seconds exposure each, the next ten at 20 seconds, and the following ten at 30 seconds. Thereafter, the exposure was increased by five seconds for each new batch of ten pictures. The successful photographs taken between 10 p.m and 10:30 p.m., received an exposure of approximately 45 seconds prior to the lights flashing. The shutter was closed as soon as the lights began to fade. In one instance, a photograph of two lights was obtained on one picture, as the second one flashed on almost immediately. His visual impression was that the discharge in each flash traveled downwards.

In an effort to make some reason out of the Brown Mountain rhyme, the *Enigma Project* joined forces with *Oak Ridge Isochronous Observation Network* (ORION) in 1978. Collectively, researchers from both groups began to take a hard look at the anomaly to better determine scientific methods of studying it. The first joint *Enigma/ORION* investigation occurred during the first week of July in 1978. Researchers converged on Brown Mountain with cameras, telescopes, communications gear, and Geiger counters. They strained their eyes every evening of that week with little or no reward for their vigilance.

Then one evening, they were gifted with a significant sighting. At precisely midnight, a rather bright diffused white light appeared among the trees on the northern slopes of Chestnut Mountain. Luckily they were prepared for the sighting, which lasted perhaps five seconds. The light performed a horizontal zigzag movement before blinking out. They managed to measure the length of the movement within the five second interval. Based on their three mile distance from the mountain, they determined that the light's approximate speed was 55 feet per second (37.5 mph). Considering that particular velocity in such rugged terrain, devoid of all but the most primitive roads, they discounted any man-made contrivance as being the cause of the strange light.

Additional observations were made and recorded by Dean Novelli during the joint *Enigma/ORION* investigation:

At 10:30 p.m. a single bluish-white light appeared on top of Chestnut Mountain at what appeared to be the immediate right (south) of the fire tower. The intensity of the light varied. It would flash brightly and dim. It would glow constantly or flash brightly and dim or both. However, no motion was observed.

Note: Observations of this light were badly hampered by a sudden influx and departure of cars at the 181 Overlook. The headlights would cause temporary night blindness and were often left on pointing out from the overlook making it impossible to see anything but illuminated haze and tops of trees a few dozen yards off. This continued to be a problem throughout the night but not to the extent that it was at this time.

At 10:35 p.m., the single light has dimmed and gone out.
Note: At this point my (Novelli) efforts to keep an accurate record of time broke down due to the duration and variety of lights and also because of the general excitement.

At 10:45 p.m. a single bluish-white light reappeared in approximately the same location. Its activities were similar to the first light observed. Aided by a pair of 7x power binoculars, he was able to see the light more clearly through the haze. He was not able to determine the top of the ridge, the skyline or the location of the fire tower.

Still looking through the binoculars, he observed a second smaller light of the same color as the other light. The second light slowly removed itself from the first, leaving a trail till it was far enough away for the two lights to be seen separately. This would be less than a half inch looking through the binoculars. The smaller light then stopped moving, dimmed and went out. Its direction was 7 o'clock from the larger light. He estimated the second lights size as not more than 1/4 the size of the first light. He observed this motion of the second light twice and estimated its duration at not more than 30 seconds.

At this time, another light attracted his attention. It was located about half way up the side of Chestnut Mountain and to the right (south) of center. Observing through binoculars, he saw a dull white glow with a green tint spread along the horizontal axis. It was beam-shaped and appeared brighter in the center. His immediate impression was that of a vehicle (jeep or motorcycle) slowly making its way across the mountain. The light first appeared near the center and moved slowly towards the right (south), there was a slight rising and falling (a shimmering or wavering) motion to the light but this could be a perception of his own.

Another light began appearing at the top of Chestnut Mountain to the right (south) of the fire tower and the first two sightings. It would flash brightly, fade and go out. The first time he saw it, it flashed red, faded to orange-red and went out. The next two times it was orange-red. He saw three flashes total (although this is not the only time it could have flashed) each lasting five seconds with ten to fifteen seconds separating the flashes. All flashes appeared to be from the same point source and the last two flashes appeared closer together with respect to time.

His attention was attracted, mainly to the comments of the group, to several dull glows similar to the single described previously. They were difficult to see without binoculars but he could tell that their position on the mountain was about half way between center and the right (south) end of the ridge. After viewing them continuously for several minutes, their position had shifted slightly toward the right (south).

Observing through the binoculars he saw up to six dull glowing lights at one time. Their color was white with a greenish tint. They were of various sizes but none were greatly out of proportion to the rest. They appeared as a horizontal group, spread about above and below the axis. Like the other light, they were beam-shaped but had a bright area in the left (north) to center of the whole shape. What proportion of the whole area the bright section made up was hard to tell. No clear distinction of the light was present to the observer.

He has estimated that the binoculars he was using have a field of view of 660 yards at 2.25 miles (the distance he estimated they observed the lights from). This would indicate that the lights were spread out over a 1/4 mile at least.

Note: These notes record only what he distinctly saw. They are in the order he saw them with the last lights going out of view at about 11:10 p.m. He was aware of their lack of a clear description of size, color, position and time. These are by no means the only things the lights could have done. He was concentrating primarily on recording the phenomenon on film and not visually. The results of his efforts were first made available for viewing at the July 27, 1978 ORION meeting. Other ORION members present at this sighting of the Brown Mountain lights were Melissa Monty, and Dave and Nancy Hackett.

There have been innumerable investigations of these lights by dozens and dozens of paranormal organizations and interested individuals. I even had a chance to view the lights from the Rt. 181 overlook and Wiseman's View. I was accompanied by a small team of investigators in 1984. At that time, I was indeed lucky to meet Mike Frizzell of the Enigma Project and Raymond D. Manners, President of International Fortean Organization (INFO). We tirelessly spent hours upon hours on that weekend in fruitless pursuit of these elusive lights. Unfortunately I "think" that I "might" have observed one very short bluish light during the entire weekend. The weather during that summer excursion there was unsettled and quite humid, even during the evening hours. The weather seems to be the determining factor in all of the investigations and sightings of these lights. Perhaps future investigations might shed some more light of these mysterious balls of light.

Buffaloe's Light:
(Directions: One mile north of the Wiccacon River on the old River Road in Hertford County)

An old time resident, Edgar Bazemore, who lived off the River Road a mile north of the Wiccacon River, quotes tradition as saying that a "buffaloe," the name given a conscription evader or deserter during the Civil War, was captured by Confederate soldiers and immediately shot. The man continued to show life. The soldiers weren't wasting any more ammunition but then seized his legs and submerged his head in a roadside spring until he had drowned.

Occasionally since that time, people have reported seeing a bright light floating in the vicinity of the old spring. Following tradition, it has always been identified as the Buffaloe's Light.

Chapanoke Light:
(Directions: Chapanoke Woods near Okisko off US Hwy 17)

A strange light has been seen across a road called Four Mile Desert. It seems to only appear on humid evenings and rises out of the swamp. It rises out of the bog and dodges the wet mossy trees, then, rising as if on a swift creek of heated air bounds down the length of the Desert Road only to vanish again in the swamp.

Chimney Rock

Scientific theory suggests the light is formed by phosphorous from the trees which is swirled into the air by rising swamp gas. The light moves through the swamp low to the ground with dimensions estimated at three feet wide and a foot deep.

Chimney Rock Pass:
(Directions: along US Hwy 74)
Lights have been reported along U.S. Highway 74 in the Blue Ridge Mountains, 25 miles southeast of Asheville.
(Source: Atlas of the Mysterious in North America by Rosemary Ellen Guiley)

Conway:

(Directions: near Conway in Northampton County along Rt. 35 and US Hwy 158)

Devil's Pocosin was a thick, dark, hazardous haven for evil spirits, together with the wildcat and panther, in colonial and antebellum times. Neglected by map-makers, it is a two-mile-long and one-mile-wide strip of flat land at the head of several swamps and river branches, southeast of Conway and northeast of Milwaukee. These include Panther Swamp, Paddy's Delight Creek and tributaries of Kirby's Creek.

Until recent years, the wet lands produced such an abundance of huckleberries that groups of pickers hazarded its thickets, the deadly cottonmouths moccasin, wildcats and panthers.

The recesses of the pocosin provided the chief haunt for the devil and the witches from nearby communities. Here they gathered and plotted wicked schemes upon the good people. The jack-o'-lantern was often seen upon the borders of the pocosin to entice men into the thickets where they would become lost and roam until daybreak, the legends had it.

Cove City Light:

(Directions: Right turn off Old Hwy 70, east at a country store and stop at third bridge on the winding rural paved road to Trenton.)

For many years there have been rumors of a strange light at Cove City. It was said that it could be seen in the early morning hours after midnight, that is, if you were at the right spot. The light has been described in many terms. Stories about the light ranged from its being a large transparent ball to a glowing sphere the size of a basketball. Rumor spread that if the light ever got in your car, it would cause you to go insane.

One experience was quite a bit scary for those involved. The group had been parked on the bridge for about forty-five minutes. Twice they had seen a glow coming towards them from about a mile away. Both times the glow had transformed into the headlights of an approaching automobile.

As the second hour of waiting approached, their anticipation changed to boredom. For the third time, a glow appeared behind them about a mile away. Most likely another car, they thought. As the light approached, now about one-half mile from them, they noticed that there were not two lights....a sign that it was not headlights. Maybe a motorcycle or a car with one headlight burned out, they reasoned.

As they remembered that night many years ago, they recalled having experienced a feeling of discomfort as the light continued to travel towards them. When it got about 300 yards away, they started the car in anticipation of leaving. With heads turned, they watched as the light slowly came closer. It was large, approximately 30 feet in diameter. As it closed in, 150 yards away, it seemed to be getting larger. The light was perfectly round and seemed to glide atop the road.

Yet is wasn't extremely bright, for they all recall that the glare did not hurt their eyes. With the engine running, the driver slipped the transmission into drive and held his foot on the brake. When the light was about 75 yards from them, he began to ease the car forward out of fear.

Instantly, the light began to recede. Slowly at first, then rapidly, so that in a matter of just a few seconds, it had become a small glowing ball. Then suddenly it was gone.

Diamond Grove:
(Directions: Located in a now remote strip of roadway connecting the Diamond Grove-Jacksonville Road with the Seaboard-Jackson Road in Northampton County.)

The late J.G. Bottoms of Margarettsville said that before this became a part of the North Carolina system and was improved, it was one of the worst pieces of roads anywhere. Bordered by flat woodlands, it was wet and muddy all winter and much of the rest of the year as well. According to local legend, only the devil experienced no difficulty in traveling the road, and it was said that he took delight in racing his black steed upon the way, henceforth the title "Devil's Racetrack".

However, the obstacles created a challenge to the amusement-loving common people when horse racing and cock fighting were the preferred sports. The gentry raced at well-known tracks like nearby Diamond Grove, Pleasant Hill and Faison's Old Tavern. The common people gathered at Devil's Racetrack with a mottled assortment of farm horses. Brandy drinking and gambling always accompanied the races, and often the event turned into a turbulent affair with swearing and fighting as a side attraction.

Eventually the sale of alcoholic beverages was prohibited in all parts of Northampton County, except at the village of Seaboard. Devil's Racetrack was a convenient link for those people coming from the southeast to visit the village's bars. Before leaving, the drinking folks invariably had "one for the road." By the time they reached Devil's Racetrack they were ready for cart, wagon or carriage racing. Hazards of the narrow way caused many vehicles to wreck, horses to run away, and people to tangle in fights. Thus the wicked reputation of the old road was kept alive, while new stories of the devil's work were spun.

Ghost lights have been reported in the narrow part of the roadway where so many people allegedly lost their lives while engaged in racing and drinking -- a dangerous mixture.

Ephriam's Light:
(Directions: near Seaboard in Northampton County along Rt. 305 and 186)

The late Mrs. Bernice Kelly Harris, a Seaboard author, quotes tradition as saying a slave by the name of Ephriam killed his master and that he paid for his deed with his life. During the ensuing years, his light has been reportedly seen time and time again near the place where he was hanged by a lynch-mob.

Hanging Tree Lights:
(Directions: Located between Williamston and Jamesville along US Hwy 64)

There are many tales about an old tree and the appearance of strange lights nearby. Many people have ascribed to the fact of visiting the tree at night and being presented by "about a thousand lights" in the heavens surrounding it.

On one occasion, two brothers saw the lights and decided to try their luck. After firing several shots towards the lights and other objects dimly seen, they decided to go home for some rope and try to lasso them. They secured the rope and returned to find the lights still glowing. They tried out their lariat, with no success whatever, and finally had to give up. They reported that the lights vanished shortly afterwards, going in the direction of the Roanoke River, which is nearby.

On another occasion, a group of reputable people said they were driving along the road near the "Hanging Tree" when the lights suddenly appeared! This time the lights came down near the roadside, then went under the wagon in which the people were riding, and hovered there for a few minutes before disappearing.

Could these lights have been the spirits of the early settlers who were murdered along the banks of the Roanoke River by Indians during the war with the Tuscaroras? Who knows?

The Maco Light:
(Directions: in Brunswick County and extreme SE corner of NC, twelve miles NW of Wilmington on US Hwy 74/76)

The Maco Light or "Joe Baldwin's Light", as it is sometimes referred to, is undoubtedly one of the most famous ghost lights seen throughout the United States. The light dates back to 1867 and was always seen along the Atlantic

Coast Line Railroad, once part of the old Wilmington-Florence-Augusta tracks. The Maco Station once occupied this area and had previously been known as Farmer's Turnout.

The rail bed where the Maco Light has been reported for generations

The story goes that Joe Baldwin was an engineer riding on a train one night on a rear coach when he suddenly realized that it had become uncoupled. Another train was following and rapidly approaching the runaway car. He knew if he didn't act quickly that a major disaster was forthcoming. So, he grabbed a signal lantern and started waving frantically from the coach's platform to try to ward off the oncoming train. The other train could not stop in time and rammed into the rear of the uncoupled car and, in the impact, severed Joe's head from his body.

Shortly after this incident, a mysterious light began to appear along the tracks near the Maco Station. Many people believed that it was the spirit of Joe Baldwin still looking for his severed head with the lantern or perhaps forever attempting to stop the oncoming train. Since that night, hundreds of people have reportedly seen the Maco light. Many unusual encounters have been reported.

The most reported phenomena seems to be a white to yellow light that comes racing up the tracks toward the observer until it gets within 75 to 100 yards away. The light then sits there and hovers, sometimes changing colors and intensity, and eventually goes racing down the track at incredible speeds away from the witnesses.

One of the most famous witnesses to the light was President Grover Cleveland, whose train paused near Maco Station in October 1894. The president said he saw two lights, one red and one green apparently being swung like a lantern. Startled, the president called the conductor to his room and inquired about the mysterious glow. The conductor smiled and said, "What you have seen, sir, is the Maco Station Light."

Ghost hunter Hans Holzer visited the spot in April of 1964 and he brought along a psychic, Ethel Myers, to help determine if the old railroad station was indeed haunted. Even though he interviewed dozens of witnesses, he never saw the light himself. However, he did come away with the belief that the area was very haunted.

The only other investigations of the light, besides a few by electronic engineers and local groups, was a professor from Duke University who tested the light a number of years ago. His opinion was that the light was indeed headlights from automobiles reflected off the highway and through the trees. He, however, could not explain why the first sightings were before the coming of the automobile.

Late in 1977, the Atlantic Coast Line tracks were torn up and dismantled because the railroad could no longer be run economically. Since that time the Maco light's appearances have been extremely rare. In fact, local residents have stated that they haven't seen the light for over 10 years. Did the workers who removed the tracks disturb the spirit of Joe Baldwin and his natural hunting ground? Hood's Trestle, which spans Hoods Creek, was removed prior to the removal of the railroad tracks. This, supposedly, was the exact spot where Joe allegedly lost his head. Local historians claim that when Hood's Trestle was removed, the lights stopped.

According to the legend, Joe's head and lantern, because of the impact, were thrown into the murk of the creek and even though Joe's body was found days later after the wreckage was cleaned up, no head was ever found. The New Hanover County Museum has on permanent display a head and lantern supposedly attributed to Joe Baldwin.

To sum all this up, we have a train wreck, a decapitation of an engineer, the appearance of ghost lights, numerous witnesses including a former president, the removal of Hood's Trestle and the railroad tracks and finally the disappearance of the lights. What does this all mean? Apparently the area was disturbed by workers and so drastically changed and altered that Joe's ghost no longer haunts the area. This is one possibility. Others suggest that because of other natural lighting in the area, the ghost light can no longer be seen. And still others claim it is because of the flora that has overgrown in the area making it impossible for stray light to enter into that area and cause the ghost light effect.

The *Ghost Research Society* arrived in the area on June 5, 1984 and talked to local residents, library personnel and people who actually saw the light years ago. All of them confirmed that the Maco light hadn't been observed for several years. Nonetheless, we spent three days in the area, walking around and making various observations at the creek and the area where the station once stood. We found nothing out of the usual, except we did discover three rusty old railroad spikes. Apparently, they were original spikes used in the building of the old tracks. We kept these as souvenirs of our visit to Maco. We did not see any strange lights at all and were disappointed -- but not all ghost hunts can be successful ones.

Even today though, the legend of Joe Baldwin and the Maco Light is alive and well. Folk singer John Golden included *The Light at Maco Station* on his album *Ballads*.

The Mintz Light:
(Directions: between Clinton and Roseboro along Rt. 24)
There is a belief that way out in the middle of nowhere, between Clinton and Roseboro, there is a ghost. Many, many people have gone just to catch a glimpse of it.

One dark, dreary night a group of youngsters decided to go and see the popular Mintz light. Some of the group had seen it before while others had not. They rode and rode and turned and turned until they came to a long dirt road. There was nothing on this road for at least a mile and then they saw a house And not just an ordinary house. It was very big and was surrounded by large trees with low-hanging branches. In short, it was eerie and looked as if it was abandoned. It was directly in front of this house that they had to wait. (One always has to wait for the light to appear.)

They were sitting on a train track that had not been in operation for years. They looked down the track and two rows of trees on either side of the rail line. The night was pitch black, and, to them, it was quite spooky sitting there between an old house and long tunnel-line of darkness. They got out of the car and just stood around waiting.

As the legend goes, a man carrying a lantern is supposed to walk down the tracks. He is the ghost of a deaf man who was walking along the tracks with a lantern years ago and was struck and decapitated. The train had blown its whistle, but the man could not hear it. Now his ghost walks up and down the train tracks, trying to find his severed head.

The group waited and waited. They were beginning to hear things. They were laughing and talking when they heard a sound. They all stopped talking and looked down the track. It sounded like someone stepping on the branches on the ground. The boys could not see anyone, but continued to hear the sound. At this time, they began, one by one, to get into the car. A few of them, however, were still standing outside.

Far down the tracks, they could see what looked like a lantern that seemed to sway ever so slightly. It was coming straight for the boys. It looked like the light of a train coming. It continued to come toward the group. Now, everyone got inside the car. They attempted to start the car, but it would not start. (That mishap is also part of the legend when the light appears.) They were now starting to panic but all of a sudden, the light disappeared.

Some say that the reason for the light is that far down the tracks there is an intersection which cars approach and then turn off. That is one explanation for the phenomenon. However, the group that saw the light that evening, heard the strange sounds and had the light simply vanish into thin air, don't believe all the so-called logical explanations. They truly believe they had a genuine encounter with the Mintz Light.

Smithfield:
(Directions: 24 miles SE of Raleigh on US Hwy 70 in Johnson County)
Spectral lights danced on Mill Creek Bridge in the 1950s. Old timers in the area say the luminescent flashes are the ghost of an old black man being lashed by his cruel master. In May 1820, Master Lynch and one of his slaves, Old Squire, were clearing land near the wooden bridge here. Lynch lashed at the slave with his whip once too many times, and the large black man struck back at his master with a hoe. Old Squire buried Lynch under the bridge, and before long, people started noticing strange things at the wooden crossing. Lanterns would go out as the bridge was crossed, and weird sound emanated from under it. Once, a man's cane was snatched from his hand as he stepped onto the bridge, only to be returned to him when he reached the other side. Old Squire confessed to the murder on his death bed.
(Source: National Directory of Haunted Places by Dennis William Hauck)

Vander:
(Directions: near Vander in Cumberland County along Rt. 24 S of Fayetteville)
The mysterious light seen recently near Vander could be nothing more then a nocturnal reflection, and it's even possible that the people who claim to have seen it are only imagining things. Harold Black, of Fayetteville, however wryly suggests there may be more going on at Vander than meet the eye.

A new chapter in North Carolina's colorful folklore may be added because of a mysterious light recently seen near Vander, in Cumberland County. The unexplainable light has caused so many curious folk to flock to the scene each night, that residents have appealed to local police to quell the noise.

Unlike the well-known Maco Light, and the Brown Mountain lights, which are somewhat unpredictable, the Vander Light is constant and can be seen any night, and at any hour.

North Carolina is rich in folk tales and ghost stories. Of the hundreds who have made the pilgrimage to view the phantom light, none have been able to pinpoint its exact location. When seen from the highway, it appears to be shining in the middle of the Atlantic Coast Line tracks an undetermined distance away, near a huge swampy area. Parties have separated and attempted to close in on the apparition from both Stedman and the Vander side of the swamp, but have been unable to see it close-up. Yet after the two groups met, they'd look back and see the ghostly gleam behind them.

As one watches the light, it occasionally rises into the air and grows dim. Falling back it reaches a new brilliance, then dims to a soft glow. This cycle repeats itself endlessly.

The phenomenon appears in an area that has been of deep interest to scientists for many years. Some years ago, *The News* and *Observer* (local newspapers) carried a story in which Harold Black related the story of the Carolina Bays, a series of shallow depressions throughout the area. These oval-shaped depressions are found by hundreds through the section. They are swampy bays and lakes, all pointing in the same direction, all oval-shaped, and all with white sandy rims. The most commonly accepted theory is that many years ago the area was bombarded by a swarm of meteors that glanced off the earth's surface, digging the oblong craters as they struck.

It is known that instruments taken in the bays have indicated magnetic variations. This, of course, reveals something's down there. It also indicates that something is likely metal.

Down in Vander, the natives are beginning to tell the worn-out story of some murdered peasant looking for his killer. Perhaps the light seen is the soul of that unfortunate murder victim endlessly wandering the area around Vander?

NORTH DAKOTA

Fargo:
(Directions: extreme eastern North Dakota in Cass County along I-29 and I-94) A single moving light has been seen along a road between Fargo and Kindred.

(Source: Atlas of the Mysterious in North America by Rosemary Ellen Guiley)

OHIO

Elmore:
(Directions: about 15 miles SE of Toledo on Woodville Road, in Sandusky County. The bridge is across the middle branch of the Portage River east of town)

A light has been seen on Woodville Road, which stretches from Toledo to Elmore. There is a bridge just into the town of Elmore and, according to locals, on a certain day in March (perhaps the 21st), if you flash your brights three times and honk your horn the same amount, the ghost of a dead motorcyclist will appear and drive straight towards your car, only to disappear just before he reaches your automobile.

There is a rather romantic story behind this one, in which a young soldier, returning from World War I, comes home to his fiancé, only to discover that she has been dating another man. In a fit of anger, he left and started down the dark, dirt road on his motorcycle. Going down the road at an accelerated speed, he collided with another car, and ever since, he has remained there. The light seen at the locale is a single light resembling that cast from a motorcycle! The story is said to date from 1918!

The other story is quite different and goes something like this:

Legend has it that many years ago there was a drunk driver driving down a dirt road. He had made a wrong turn and was lost. There were very few houses on this road and it was hardly ever traveled. There was a farm house though and a young boy about 8 or 9-years-old lived there with his family. He was outside playing after dark and was hit by the drunk driver. The driver turned off his engine and flashed his headlights three times to see if the boy would move. When he didn't the driver got scared and drove off.

The boy's father noticed the headlights flashing and ran out to see what was going on. All he saw though was the rear end of the car as it drove away. He called for his son and when there was no answer he went in and got a lantern and began to search for him. He found him laying in the road.

So, now the legend has it that if you go to the place where the boy was killed, turn off your engine and blink your headlights three times, a bright light will come out of nowhere and start heading for your car. The boy was allegedly killed around midnight, so they also say if you stay there until midnight, the light will pass through your car making it explode. I guess I wouldn't want to test the latter story!

Loudonville:

(Directions: Rt. 3, and Rt. 39, SE of Mansfield. Nearby Mohican Memorial State Forest probably woods where light is seen)

A single stationary light has been reported by local residents in a wooded area near here this location. Originally seen on the Glen Zimmerman farm, along a rural road, this light doesn't appear every night but it always follows the same route across the field and into a woods at the foot of a slope. For many years this light appeared, floating about four feet above the ground, bobbing and swaying slightly. Mrs. Zimmerman once said it appeared as if someone were carrying a lantern, and it moves at about the speed of a walking man -- only there was never a man. There was only the open field, often bathed in bright moonlight, and the light moving along its unchangeable course.

Oxford Light:

(Directions: located near Miami University on Rt. 73 and Rt. 732, NW of Cincinnati, in Butler County)

The story surrounding this light is that a young man was racing on his motorcycle to meet his girlfriend and to ask for her hand in marriage. It was raining and dark and this road is very hilly with a sharp curve at the end. A tractor was coming around the curve and saw the man on the motorcycle coming and flashed his lights to warn him to stop. The young man could not stop in time and was killed instantly (some say decapitated, of course).

Now, they say you can go to the top of the street where the tractor was and flash your lights. Soon, you will see a light coming towards you, appearing and disappearing as it crests the hills. Then, the light disappears a few hills from you. You never hear the motor of what seems to be a phantom vehicle, just see a light. One witness claimed the light passed right through his car without incident!

OKLAHOMA

Ada:

(Directions: 70 miles SE of Oklahoma City on Rt. 1 and Rt. 3)

A red globe of light occasionally bounds up on unsuspecting witnesses here. The lights were reported by John Bennett of the *Ada Evening News* back in November 1962. Part of his report is as follows:

"It looked orange, like light filtering through the trees from a window of a house. 'That's just a house light,' I scoffed. The boys and girls (watching the nightly show) answered in chorus that if that was a house light, it was the first one they ever had seen that danced and changed colors. And, by golly, it did.

"It started glowing bigger and bigger and giving off a diffused orange, then red, then yellow light. For a full five minutes the light glowed like a dying ember. Then things started happening.

"The lights began to dance. They flickered eerily up and down like a bouncing luminous ball, then darted sideways. The single ball of light appeared about three feet in diameter....During its fantastic flight back and forth it changed colors: first orange, then yellow, then red. But it stayed in one general area, behind what looked like a sparse growth of trees....

"In the tree line the light had changed colors again and was beginning to get more active. Suddenly a piece of the glow broke away and started a rapid bouncy course across the field in front of us. It looked like a luminous basketball, and about the same size. It danced before our eyes about 100 yards out front. We traced the glowing trajectory that appeared like a giant lightning bug, until it went out...

"The big show ended there. Shortly after the field orbit by the satellite the glow resumed but it didn't dance around much. In about an hour I left. My suspicion is that it is a hoax but I can't explain the dancing lights. It would take a clever manipulation of light. And it's beyond me how anyone could make the darn thing go so fast."

Kenton:
(Directions: far western panhandle of Oklahoma on Rt. 325)

A single moving light was reported about eight miles east of Kenton, plus another different single moving light approximately 15 miles southwest of the town.

(Source: Atlas of the Mysterious in North America by Rosemary Ellen Guiley)

Peoria:
(Directions: far NE Oklahoma on Rt. 10)

A ghostly white glow has been hovering over this northeastern Oklahoma town for many years. The light typically appears about five miles northeast of the town and can be seen from a distance along a three-mile stretch of road running westward from Missouri. One local believer says the light passed right over his head, bright enough to read by, and disappeared when he honked his car horn.

Most of the legends about the Peoria lights center around decapitation. One story says the light is that of a luckless Indian who fell victim to his ax-swinging wife. Another says the light is a miner who lost his head in an accident. A third says it is a Civil War soldier left headless when he was hit between the eyes with a cannonball. Bob Whitebird, a former chief of the nearby Quapaw tribe, reports that a Seneca Indian did lose his head via the ax in a domestic dispute many years before. Then there are those who say the lights are the spirits of young Indian lovers who leapt to their deaths when they could not marry.

The lights can be dangerous, but only to local residents and onlookers. One man claims the troublemakers out at the viewing spot make the area unsafe, although sheriff's deputies patrol the road. Farmer Chester McMinn would not go down into the pasture at night to milk the cows, fearing someone would see him swinging lantern and take a potshot at the lights. McMinn admitted that he did some scaring of his own, however. He would drive his 1948 Chevrolet right up to the parked cars of the onlookers and turn on a spotlight he had mounted on top. Everyone would run and scream.

(Source: Atlas of the Mysterious in North America by Rosemary Ellen Guiley)

Sand Springs:
(Directions: W of Oklahoma City on Cimarron Turnpike)

It seems that the Sand Springs ghost light is a well researched, established phenomenon. The September 27, 1954 issue of the *Tulsa World* carries a write-up on the Sand Springs ghost light. Although it is not an AP report it is apparently the report that the AP picked up.

The article states that the light had appeared for five consecutive nights at 12:05 a.m. It was described as a "fiery blue-green object with a phosphorescent glow. It would remain stationary at one spot for a while, go out, and then reappear a second later at least 200 yards away. It reportedly appears in the east and streaks westward at incredible speed." One woman claimed to have heard the light scream. Another witness said the light "started out as green then turned red then white." Sand Springs police chief Jack Daniels said he thought it was either a piece of metal on the hillside reflecting the moonlight or "fox fire" (luminescent fungi). Daniels said as many as 150 cars were parked along the highway nightly with their occupants gazing skyward.

The next day's *Tulsa World*, for September 28, 1954, contained a report that apparently the AP didn't pick up. It's headline read "Ghost Light at Sand

Springs Fades: Teen-age Pranksters Are Unmasked."

Two teen-age boys admitted to highway patrol deputies early that morning, at the scene of the ghost light sightings, that the whole thing was a practical joke started to impress their girl friends. For the past five nights, the boys had disguised a flashlight with a green cloth and ran through the underbrush. The boys were going to repeat their performance the morning of the 28th, but became scared when people carrying guns showed up to see the light. "Both boys' legs were badly scratched where they had raced across the face of the mountain in the brambles and rocks to carry out their scheme." The ghost light did not appear after the boys' confession.

The entire event was a hoax, but the resolution of the case appeared only in a local newspaper. The moral is: always check as close as possible to the original source when researching paranormal activity, and always check a few issues after the first appearance of the report.

OREGON

<u>La Grande:</u>
(Directions: Blue Mountains, N of La Grande along State Hwy 204)

On a mid-January night in 1955, a deep snow covered the Blue Mountains north of La Grande, Oregon. Along the Weston-Elgin road Manuel Erickson, accompanied by Barney Thompson, was operating a State Highway Department snow plow. Suddenly, several hundred yards ahead of them, the two men saw a strange blue light about two feet in diameter. Erickson dimmed the light of the truck. There was no change in the light, which continued coming toward the plow above the highway.

Bewildered, Erickson stopped and so did the blue light. "It seemed to be looking at us," one of the men said later. After a half a minute or so, the light began moving up, down and sideways. Finally, with a humming sound, it moved upward and disappeared behind some trees. Erickson started up and the light reappeared on the other side of the road. It emitted several blue flashes, then vanished.

A week later, Robert Backus, another night-time plow driver, stopped to check his chains. As he stood beside his vehicle, he noticed with some surprise that he was casting a shadow. He looked up: overhead was the bobbing blue light, and from it came a humming noise.

Backus said he started up and the light followed him "a little way," then it moved in a leisurely way down a canyon until it was out of sight. A number of other residents in the area told reporters of the *La Grande Evening Observer* that they had seen the light.

<u>Wasco:</u>
(Directions: just off US Hwy 197 S of Dalles, in Wasco County)
Strange floating lights are seen in the area of the John Day River, as well as the ghost of an old lady with long white hair. It seems that Mary Leonard and her husband often robbed wealthy guests who stayed at their hotel back in the 1880s and buried their bodies nearby. Mary was jailed for killing her own husband and when she was finally released, she was said to have spent the remaining years of her life searching the riverbank for the buried loot that they had stolen from their murder victims. Allegedly, the lights seen here is the ghost of Mary Leonard either still looking for her gold or attempting to scare others away from finding it.

PENNSYLVANIA

<u>Buckingham:</u>
(Directions: Hansell Road between Buckingham and Pipersville on Rt. 413 in Bucks County)
Hansell Road is an innocent-looking rural road, except for the reports of what goes on there after dark. The stories include a glowing green light that can be seen in the woods next to the road, swinging as if it were a lantern being held by someone. Some say the light works it way towards onlookers thru the woods. The light appears to grow larger and larger and often hovers when it finally reaches the road! One report even went as far to say that it hovered for a few seconds then proceeded to "drop" straight down and splatter on the road; resembling the same effect as a drop of water falling into a puddle. Sometimes, it then rises from the road and begins to roll toward those unfortunate enough to still be around from it's previous display. It finally rolls away into the deep woods on either side of Hansell Road.

The best way to see the light, is of course, finding the correct road. It's a short road. Turn off your headlights and engine. Legend has it that you won't see the light with the car lights on or engine running.

There have been reports as close as 50 feet away from the light, which took the shape of a 6-foot tall cylinder. That particular sighting only lasted between 3-5 seconds while others have seen the light for several minutes at a time.

One legend for the light's appearance is that a slave was killed on the road. There is also a overhead streetlight nearby that seems to wink off when people approach. They say this is because the road is haunted. The road was recently paved and, according to locals, the light hasn't been seen as much as when the road was dirt.

Witches' Hill:
(Directions: the hill runs between Virginville and Windsor Castle in Williams Township. Follow Hexenkopf Road along the bluff, which overlooks Stout Valley. The area is W of Allentown and N of Reading)
What we know today as crop circles were called *Hexen Danz* by the Pennsylvania Dutch. These flattened circles of wheat were blamed on dancing witches. This mountain was where the witches gathered, especially on May 1st , or Walpurgis Nacht. Their phantoms along with strange balls of light, are still seen on this hilltop, which locals call *Hexenkopf*, or Witches' Head.

RHODE ISLAND

Block Island:
(Directions: located almost due S of Providence in the Block Island Sound)
About 11 miles off Long Island between Montauk and Gay Head, people sometimes see the outline of a ship during Christmas week, apparently on fire. Sometimes simply seen as a luminous white or likened to a great red fireball on the ocean.

It is thought to be the *Palatine*, a German schooner, that was ferrying religious outcasts to New York at the end of the 18th Century, when she met the same fate that others before had. The Block Island lighthouse is supposed to keep sailing ships away from the dangerous Black Rock, which has wrecked many a ship in the past. Some simply see the strange light at sea, while others have professed to have actually seen the unfortunate victims onboard burning to death and have heard their anguished cries for help.

In 1969, dozens of witnesses described a great fireball in the ocean, and, to this day, the light from the burning *Palatine* is reported by residents of Block Island. John Greenleaf Whittier penned a long poem about the Palatine Light, which concludes:

"Now low and dim, now clear and higher/Leaps up the terrible Ghost of Fire/Then, slowly sinking, the flames expire/And wise Sound skippers, though

skies be fine/Reef their sails when they see the sign/Of the blazing wreck of the Palatine!"

SOUTH CAROLINA

Bingham's Light:
(Directions: in Dillion off I-95 Dillion exit and at the Historical Marker is a dirt road that leads into the woods. Park and walk about a mile)

It is said that after you park your car at this site, you should walk about a mile into the woods and begin yelling for the light to appear. You will know when you are close to seeing the light because the temperature will drop.

According to legend, John Bingham was hit by a train in the late 1800s or early 1900s, depending who you ask in town. He was flagging the train with a lantern and apparently it's his lantern that is still seen today swaying back and forth. The train tracks no longer exist.

One report claims that the light got to within three feet of the onlooker and he got violently ill, another claims his engine blew up when the light got too close and still another claims to have shot at the light with a rifle. The light split and changed into different colors.

Land's End Light:
(Directions: on St. Helen's Island near the town of Frogmore)

The light was first sighted in 1948 and is described as a ball of fire, which appears near the Chapel of Ease. Dee Fitzsimmons, a policewoman at Hilton Head Island, saw the light in 1982 and described it a fiery flash, which passed right through the car ahead of her and quickly dart to the right, where it was lost in the woods.

Legends abound that the light could be the ghost of a Confederate soldier who was decapitated during the Civil War and still continues to look for his disembodied head! Another tale tells of a busload of workers coming home late one evening, when the driver, apparently distracted for a brief moment, crashed the bus into a hug oak tree nearby.

The best place to view the light is near an old cemetery and the only remaining upright mausoleum. Some claim the light actually bounces on the road like an oversized beach ball. The light is often seen as a large ball of fire with a reddish halo rimming the central light.

Whatever locals say the light may be, it continues to baffle those who come here each year to catch a glimpse of this mysterious phenomena.

Ravenel:
(Directions: 20 miles W of Charleston, on US Hwy 165 just S of US Hwy 17)

The story goes that there were three teenage boys who were run over by a logging truck on an empty stretch of road about twenty miles west of Charleston. They are buried behind a Baptist Church located along the same road. It is said that if you knock on the church door three times and say, "We want to see the light," and then repeat this process three times, the lights would appear to you on the stretch of road where the boys had been killed.

A newcomer to the area was told of the lights, and became curious to see them for himself, or to see if there was any truth to the story. So one night he went to the church with some friends at about 11:30 p.m. He went through the whole knocking procedure, and then they all went back out to the road to wait for the lights. There were several cars already parked on the side of the road, and a few came out of the church-yard after they did. About 12:30 a.m., his friends in the car all started to become very excited. At the same time, the cars in front of them all took off. The newcomer looked up the road and saw only what appeared to be a car (from a distance, the two headlights of a car appeared to be one light -- this "one light" was what he saw). He yelled, "It's just a car." His friends were visibly shaken though and one in the passenger seat just pointed down the road toward the light. When he looked again, the light had separated, not into two lights, but three lights. They were lined up side by side, like three motorcycles getting ready to race. After that, the newcomer quickly sped to his car and they left the area in haste!

Summerville:
(Directions: NW of Charleston along Hwy 27 and Hwy 61)

This light was first discovered in December 1961 along what was once Sheep Island Road. According to reports by the *Charlotte News* in mid-March of 1962, the light apparently enjoyed chasing automobiles down Sheep Island Road at speeds approaching 60 MPH. It was said to change colors and often liked to swoop down on parked cars.

TENNESSEE

Chapel Hill:
(Directions: central Tennessee, 15 miles S of Murfreesboro on US Alternate Hwy 31. The light is seen near a dirt road that takes a sharp dip as it crosses

the L & N tracks west of town, Depot Street)

In the 1890s, an engineer for the Louisville & Nashville Railroad was killed here. Apparently, he fell from the train as it sped around a sharp curve and was decapitated. Every night at 9:30 p.m., the L & N freight train passes this same area and soon after the train departs, a light appears that sways back and forth. According to legend, it's the headless engineer still searching for his head!

Railroad tracks in Chapel Hill where the Ghost Lights are Witnessed

Most people say that the light is not supernatural and is nothing more than the reflection of trucks' headlights bouncing off the smooth steel rails. Others attribute the light to foxfire or swamp gas, while diehard skeptics simply dismiss the light altogether as the product of overactive imaginations.

In the late 1930s, a local man named Skip Adgent was struck and killed by a train at the crossing where the light has been seen. Soon after his death others began seeing strange light at the crossing where Adgent died. Some local residents claim the light didn't begin appearing until after the murder of a Mrs. Ketchum though. She apparently disappeared from her rural home near Chapel Hill in late December of 1940. The body was later allegedly found through the aid of a Shelbyville psychic, Mr. Simon Warner. He described in detail where the body could be found and it was exact, according to the story.

In the 1970s, four witnesses saw the light pass through a car stalled on the tracks. The light always grows dimmer when it moves thorough an object.

I visited the site and attempted to find the exact viewing location. After several hours of wandering around, I flagged down a Chapel Hill Police officer and asked for directions. He gave them to me but warned that if I was actually caught on the tracks, that he would have to arrest me for trespassing. Apparently, a number of people have been killed looking at what they thought was the ghost light, only to be killed by an approaching train! So the railroad officials told the police to arrest anyone seen walking the tracks. They wanted to make the location off-limits and therefore safer for all.

I did sneak back there but was sure to stay off the tracks. After several hours of waiting, seeing nothing, I left disappointed.

Obed River:
(Directions: where Obed River crosses I-40)

Just yards away from where the Obed River and Interstate 40 meet, a horrible triple murder took place. Now, three mysterious balls of light are frequently seen gliding over the river valley, sometimes crossing I-40, and then disappearing into the river on the other side. These lights are said to be the souls of three men, a trapper and the two men who murdered him almost a century ago. The lights are sometimes said to emanate a curious sputtering sound, like the live end of a dangling electric wire.

The Springville Light:
(Directions: along US Hwy 70 near US Hwy 641 in NW Tennessee, near the town of Camden)

In a small community just outside of Camden, there is an abandoned railroad bed that is now just a gravel road where railroad tracks used to be located. The story goes that during the Civil War era, a man who origin was unknown was walking along the tracks when he was struck by a train and decapitated.

To see the light you must drive down this road for some distance and turn off your vehicle's lights, and then you will see a light flickering in the distance that will slowly move toward your car. Recent reports have indicated a bright yellow light that filled the tunnel-shaped road and then disappeared. Others have watch the lantern light move toward them as a bright flash of red light appeared. Apparently, the light still makes its appearance known along this stretch of road and sightings continue today.

TEXAS

Anson Lights:
(Directions: take I/20 W from Dallas/Ft. Worth approx. 160 miles to Abilene. Once you reach Abilene, take State Highway 277 N 20 miles to Anson)

The Anson lights are supposed to be a ghost of a woman from the 1800s who is looking for her lost son. Outside of Anson there is a cemetery. About a quarter of a mile down the dirt road running along side the cemetery there is a cross roads. In order to see the lights, you are supposed to go to the cross roads and turn around and then flash your lights, turn them off and wait.

Twinkling, flickering lights are then seen on the horizon that dance down the road towards the onlookers in their cars, sometimes approaching as close as 50 feet! Rumor has it if the light gets too close to your car and you become too frightened, all you need do is turn on the cars headlights and the light will mysteriously vanish!

Bailey's Light:
(Directions: 35 miles W of Angleton on US Hwy 288 and Hwy 35 in Brazoria County)

Many say that the first appearance of this light dates back to the 1850s and is attributed to a man named Brit Bailey who died in 1832. The light allegedly rose from an old grave on the prairie's edge. In 1939, reports were accumulated that say the light was a glowing, basketball-shaped orb hovering near Bailey's Prairie. But according to local legend it appears in seven year intervals; 1946, 1953, 1960, etc., so it should appeared again in 2002.

Brit Bailey came to Texas from Kentucky in 1821. He served the area as an Indian fighter in the 1824 Battle of Jones Creek against the Karankawas and also fought in the 1832 Battle of Velasco, the first fight between Americans and Mexican troops. Within a few months, he took to his bed and later died from cholera. In his will, he stated that he wished to be buried feet-first into an eight-foot shaft. So, he actually stands in his grave!

According to the 1939 sighting reported in *Ford Times*, a Robert Munson, an insurance dealer, saw the strange light in the fall on a damp, drizzling night.

"About 150 yards away", he related, "I saw a ball of reddish-orange fire, slightly bigger than a basketball, moving in and out of the trees. My brother Joe came out and we chased the fireball for a long time, but never got close to it. It stayed just ahead of us, shooting to the top of the trees, then back down to our cattle pen and out the other side. The cattle were in a frenzy."

Then Bailey's Light floated out of the woods and headed for the highway, along which a lone automobile happened to be traveling. The brothers watched as the ball of fire bore down on the hood of the car, which swerved, then sped away.

They continued chasing the light until it finally disappeared across a bayou and into the glade where Bailey was buried. They also both saw the light again during its seven-year appearance in 1946.

Bengie's Light:
(Directions: somewhere in West Texas)

Legend has it that a mysterious light appears on a dirt road off the main highway, alongside a cemetery. Allegedly, when the town was just a pioneer settlement, several Comanche's pillaged the town and took off with a young infant. The light seen today is supposed to be the light of the lantern that the ghostly mother carries around looking for her child.

You have to drive to the crossroads, turn around and face the direction you just came from. Then, you blink your headlights and you might begin to see a strange glow on the horizon in front of you. The light begins to get closer and closer and consequently brighter and brighter. Sometimes the light displays unusual gyrations and seems almost out of control in its movement. However, this author wasn't able to obtain an exact location of this road or where the light is seen.

Big Bend National Park:
(Directions: in Brewster County. Follow US Hwy 385 S 98 miles from I-10 at Fort Stockton. Bruja Canyon cuts through Mesa de Anguilla)

Bruja Canyon (Spanish for witch) was thought to have been haunted for many years. Unexplained flickering lights are sometimes observed here as well as cameras not functioning for inexplicable reasons.

(Source: National Directory of Haunted Places by Dennis William Hauck)

Big Thicket:
(Directions: east Texas near Saratoga, 39 miles W of Beaumont on Hwy 787, N of Hwy 105 in Hardin County. Bragg Road is an eight-mile-long dirt pathway through a thicket that lies between the Neches and Trinity rivers)

This light is seen on a road locally known as Bragg Road and legend has it that Confederate General Braxton Bragg (1817-1876) once lived on this road when the trains still ran. One night a train ran over him, cutting off his head. The light is supposed to be his ghost returning to search for his missing head. Of course, this is the same basic story that is generally heard about any ghost light. In this case, the only truth to it is that Bragg did indeed live there while he was an executive for the railroad. However, he died in Galveston of natural causes. Another story is that of an ill-fated brakeman, Jake Murphy, who was beheaded by the wheels of a passing train.

All those who claim to have seen this light describe it as a moving glow, generally red, which changes in intensity from a soft luminosity to a bright, white light. Its movement varies greatly from a slow, slow glide, just barely moving, to racing like the wind, darting back and forth across the road and jumping through the trees. Sometimes it reverses its direction and other times it approaches from one direction, disappears, and reappears approaching from the opposite direction.

It once perched itself on the windshield of a parked car panicking those inside the vehicle. The *Skeptical Inquirer*, Vol. 16, Summer 1992 believed the lights to be an optical illusion caused by the lay of the land and approaching and receding cars going up and down steep hills which cause the light.

The *National Geographic*, October 1974 went to the site to see for themselves what all the fuss was about. Local religious persons call this area Holy Ghost Thicket and some get a mysterious, supernatural feeling upon entering the thicket. The viewing location is said to be approximately five miles north of Hwy 105 on Hwy 787. Another article was written about the light by *Fate* magazine in May of 1961. In 1960, Sheriff Whit Whitaker had to post orders prohibiting firearms in the area. Some of the onlookers were attempting, unsuccessfully, of course to shoot the lights out of the air.

In 1989, Professor Yoshi-Hiko Ohtsuki visited the area and attempted to photograph and videotape the strange lights. Heavy rains prevented them from seeing the lights however their investigation was carried on the Nippon Television Network in April of that year.

Blue Light Cemetery:
(Directions: located near Barrett Cemetery in Titus County in Mt. Pleasant)

Reports from local teens indicated a bluish light chased them from the cemetery area. The light appeared the moment they entered into the cemetery and when it began to move towards them, they all fled the scene. As more and more people began to report seeing the blue light at what they dubbed "Blue Light Cemetery," police officers began patrolling the cemetery property more diligently. Some people claimed they went there numerous times and never saw it, while others saw it each and every time they visited.

Some say it's simply the reflection off of the tombstones, but what could cause the reflection is anyone's guess.

In the late 1970s, a large coal company bought up all the land surrounding the cemetery and put up a gate that blocks entry into the cemetery unless you request a key to visit deceased loved ones. As you might have already guessed, the sightings have become few and far between.

Lufkin:
(Directions: along US Hwy 59 and US Hwy 69)
A single moving light has been spotted along a railroad track in the area.

(Source: Atlas of the Mysterious in North America by Rosemary Ellen Guiley)

Marfa Lights:
(Directions: seen on the Mitchell Flats, about 12 miles E of Marfa on Hwy 67 between Marfa and Alpine)

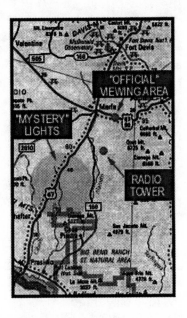

The earliest known encounter with the Marfa Lights dates back to 1883, when 16-year-old Robert Ellison was driving cattle through Paisano Pass, just west of the town of Alpine, onto Mitchell Flats. Far to the southeast are the Chinati Mountains and he saw what he believed to be the flickering flames of Apache Indian campfires in the distance.

Most observers report one or more brightly twinkling lights just after dusk, either just below or slightly above the outlined horizon. The most often described color is a greenish-yellow or yellowish-green. These lights have been seen dividing and splitting into several smaller orbs.

One of the most famous sightings of the lights occurred March 14-June 16, 1973 when two geologists, Elwood Wright and Pat Kenney, observed two lights and tried to track them down. At first they used a jeep, then later proceeded on foot. They never caught up with them, but the scientists were left with the unnerving impression that the lights were toying with them.

On March 19th, Wright and Kenney went to the air base entrance at approximately 8:30 p.m. to try to determine if what they had seen the night before were car lights. They only stayed fifteen to twenty minutes because this was long enough to convince them that they were not car lights, at least not all of them. They observed three lights moving rapidly in all directions but still in the direction of the Chinati Mountains. The lights still appeared to be at a great distance. One of the lights began swinging in an arc, like a rocker on a rocking chair. Another did a complete loop and approached the rocking light. They appeared to be playing with one another.

The next night was even more amazing! It was a fairly moonlit night and they could see the road without headlights so they left them off. They drove back toward the highway until they were about one and a half miles south of

A highway sign leading visitors to the viewing area for the Marfa Lights

the highway. They stopped at a high place on the road, turned off the engine and waited.

Three horses, about 200 feet west of the car, suddenly started running and acting in a wild manner. At this precise moment, they observed two lights moving rapidly from the southwest to the northeast, almost at right angles to the road. The first light slowed down near the road, crossed the road less than 1000 feet in front of their car, and continued to the east where it seemed to merge with or met a third light, which was brighter and was between their car and the vicinity of the old air base hanger. It crossed the road only three or four feet off the ground. The second light coming from the southwest followed approximately the same path as the first light but it seemed to be moving slower.

They decided to try to sneak up on it in the car with the lights out, and try to intercept it at the same place with the first light had crossed the road, but they could not get close to it. They could tell they were within 500-700 feet of it but it started veering to the north and when they got to the point where the first light had crossed the road, the second light was several hundred feet on down the road. They could tell how far away it was because it was only about three feet off the ground and it went behind some bushes and in front of other bushes. They could have measured the distance with a surveyors chain. The second light was not more than 200 feet from them when it crossed the road. They stopped the car and turned off the engine as it came to the edge of the road.

It moved out to the middle of the road and hovered there. They both had the distinct impression that it knew exactly where they were and that it was just daring them to chase it. The intensity of the light decreased as it slowed down and hovered in one spot. The color was approximately the same as an ordinary incandescent household light bulb. It seemed to possess intelligence!

They did not move and after approximately one-half minute it moved on to the east to join the other lights, then they all vanished. The light they observed closest appeared to be about half the size of a basketball.

Professor Yoshi-Hiko Ohtsuki from Tokyo's Waseda University videotaped the lights for 10 seconds in 1989 during a taping of *Unsolved Mysteries*, hosted by Robert Stack. These are perhaps the most famous and reoccurring lights in the country today.

San Antonio:
(Directions: I-35 and I-10 in south-central Texas)
Strange ghost lights have been reported on the outskirts of town.
(Source: Atlas of the Mysterious in North America by Rosemary Ellen Guiley)

Thorndale:
(Directions: east-central Texas, 30 miles E of Round Rock on US Hwy 79, off I-35 N of Austin. The old Snively-Pope cabin is just outside of town on the banks of the San Gabriel River)

The banks of this river are haunted by a ghost of man protecting his hidden loot that he stole. After a band of outlaws discovered that they were being followed by Texas Rangers, they broke into the cabin and killed the old man who resided there. They dug a hole for their booty and buried the victim in the same hole.

Soon, a strange yellow light was seen moving between the cabin and the riverbank. Many believe it is the ghost of the unfortunate victim guarding the treasure.

Wimberley Lights:
Wimberley, Texas is a small jewel in the Texas hill country along Cypress Creek. The creek runs from the main swimming hole down to a secluded little natural pool. A trail then runs alongside the creek to the little pool and this is the area where the lights have been seen. The campground is lined on one side by a hundred year old rock wall, and across a small dirt road is a very old cemetery.

One report mentioned the air becoming somewhat "thicker" all of a sudden and the sounds from the nearby woods died away at once. Down the path came three identical gold glowing spheres of light. They followed the course of the path and whizzed right past the onlookers and made absolutely no sound at all.

VERMONT

Stowe:

(Directions: north central Vermont, 60 miles E of Burlington. Take I-84 to the Colbyville and go N 26 miles on Hwy 100. The bridge spans Gold Brook on Gold Brook Road, a few miles outside of town)

Emily's Bridge, as it is called by locals, is a covered bridge built in 1844 and is allegedly named after the ghost that haunts it. Emily Smith was supposedly either trampled by horses, killed herself by jumping from the bridge or hanging herself from a beam.

Many say that Emily's ghost manifests as a flickering white light that drifts mysteriously around and on the bridge itself. Sometimes cold breezes are also encountered when the light is seen.

(Source: National Directory of Haunted Places by Dennis William Hauck)

VIRGINIA

Belfast Lights:

(Directions: near Rt. 19 in Belfast)

This light was seen particularly before much of the land in this region became developed and the population increased. At the time these lights were seen the most, the land involved was mostly farm and cattle grazing land. The sighting area is divided by one main road, a two-lane paved highway and Rt. 19. In Belfast, there is a particular hollow that runs from the base of Clinch Mountain, bottoming out in the valley below. This particular hollow has at least two very old graveyards, one in particular, the final resting place of several children who died in an influenza epidemic at the turn of the century.

Also, lower down in this hollow, is a house that was witness to it's own particular horror. There, a man decapitated his father-in-law with an ax during a heated argument. Some distance above the mentioned graveyards, there is the ruins of an old home where another murder took place. This time the cat was carried out by brother against brother after one caught the other with the first one's wife in a compromising situation.

For quite a number of years there has been a ball of light, about the size of a beach ball, that could be seen making its way down the hollow to the public road area at the mouth. There witnesses have sworn that they have been pursued, sometimes at great speed, by this ball of light, only to have it vanish without a trace after about a mile or so.

A couple was making their way along Route 19 and as they approached the above area, one of the riders noticed what appeared to be a floating ball of light coming across the field in their direction. They slowed the car to get a better look at the blue-white ball and the orb made it's way closer until it seemed to hover just behind their car.

Becoming spooked, they took off, gaining speed as they went, only to have the light follow at a steady distance behind. They reached speeds of over 50 MPH. The orb kept pace and even gained ground on the fleeing passengers. After a moment, the orb rose slightly, and passed over the top of their car, to hang suspended over the hood, keeping pace steadily with the moving car. No matter how fast they drove, it kept up, seeming to float stationary above the hood of the car. Then suddenly, the orb vanished; like turning out a light, and there was no trace of it's ever being there.

Blue Ridge Mountains:
Numerous ghost lights and mysterious glows are reported throughout the mountain areas.

(Source: Atlas of the Mysterious in North America by Rosemary Ellen Guiley)

Cohoke Light:
(Directions: near Salisbury in King William County. It is located at the head of the York River, at the junction of Highways 33 and 30. Take Exit 220 from I-64)

The Southern Railroad tracks in King William County have been the scene of a dull yellow to reddish glowing light. This mysterious light appears in West Point, Virginia at a place called the Cohoke Crossroads. It is described as a yellow light that moves along the railroad tracks at the crossroads. The light has been known to break up in front of an observer and reform behind him. The light is now on private property, and perhaps that's why newer accounts of this light are hard to find.

There are two stories about the light. One claims that the light is from the lantern of a headless railway worker who was killed along the tracks. The other legend centers around a phantom train that apparently disappeared during the Civil War while carrying wounded soldiers.

Kelly's Ford:
(Directions: Culpepper County)
According to legend, more than $50,000 in gold and silver coins are being

guarded near here by an eerie spook light. On September 24, 1863, Rebel soldiers were camped at this site, planning on crossing the river the next morning, when they were surprised by Union troops that killed all but four Confederates. The four escapees then buried the payroll so it wouldn't fall into the enemies' hands. They assumed that they could later retrieve the money after the danger had passed however the four were later killed in a skirmish.

The money was never recovered and locals sometimes see a yellow light moving over the site where the treasure was probably buried every month on the third and sixth days of the new moon. Witnesses say that you can never get close to the light itself, so the exact location of this buried treasure remains a mystery to this day.

Suffolk:
(Directions: S of Suffolk along Jackson Road and US Hwy 32, near the Great Dismal Swamp in Nansemond County)

Two mysterious lights, which sometimes look like one, appear here and when approached, they veer off the road and reappears behind the observer. The first sightings of the lights date back over 75 years ago. These lights were reported in an UP dispatch on March 13, 1951 and AP releases in March and April of 1951. Over 300 people showed up on one night to view the lights. Deputy Sheriff Beale related that a railroad flagman was killed in about 1912.
(Source: Mysterious Fires and Lights by Vincent H. Gaddis)

WASHINGTON

Ringold:
(Directions: seen near Pasco on US Hwy 395 near I-182)

A single moving light which resembles an automobile with a single headlight has been reported here a number of years. Reports abound of onlookers in cars actually being forced off the road and into ditches by the oncoming light. According to observations, it only appears on foggy, rainy nights.
(Source: Mysterious Fires and Lights by Vincent H. Gaddis)

Yakima Indian Reservation:
(Directions: south-central Washington, at the junction of I-82 and US Hwy 12. Much of the activity has been reported near Toppenish and White Swan)

Orange or yellow lights, which sometimes split apart while bouncing along the ground, have been seen here for many years. Local first thought these to be UFOs or extraterrestrial spacecraft of some kind. The heyday was between 1972 and 1974, when many campers and forest rangers reported observing this phenomena.

Similar lights have been observed along fault lines and just prior to earthquakes leaving scientists to believe these lights are caused by piezoelectric effect of quartz crystals rubbing together under extreme pressure causing this display. These resemble glowing baseballs of light sometimes floating along the treetops near the Cascade Mountain range.

(Source: National Directory of Haunted Places by Dennis William Hauck)

WEST VIRGINIA

Moorefield:
(Directions: on Rt. 55 and Rt. 220. Cole Mountain is located just S of town and the best views are from Hwy 55)

The Moorefield Mystery Light located just outside of the town of Moorefield, West Virginia and makes quite regular appearances. The orange-red light seen on Cole Mountain has mystified people since the middle of the nineteenth century. This ball of light bobs up and down over the mountainside. No one has gotten close to the luminous ball, and most sightings take place from the road at the base of the mountain.

Legend says the light is from the lantern of an old slave who worked on the Charles Jones plantation. The loyal slave disappeared on the side of the mountain during a raccoon hunt and was never seen again.

(Source: The National Directory of Haunted Places by Dennis William Hauck)

WISCONSIN

Oconto:
(Directions: right off Green Bay on US Hwy 41 and Rt. 22)

In the fall of 1964, a group of deer hunters were hunting in the woods just south of Oconto. At around 4 p.m. they decided to call it a day and began walking towards their cars when they heard a shot ring out in the distance. They both saw two balls of fire in the sky traveling west. At first they thought these could be tracer rounds from a rifle. However, they soon changed directions and headed right for the hunters! They were approximately 500 feet above the ground. One of the hunters tried to view them through his rifle scope and what he saw was two fireballs about the size of a medium pumpkin and roughly about 50 yards apart from one another.

They continued flying east until they disappeared into a thick bank of trees. The entire scenario lasted only about 20 seconds.

WYOMING

Newcastle:
(Directions: extreme eastern Wyoming along US Hwy 85 and US Hwy 16)
In the 1940s, ghost lights were reported near here that rolled over the ground like tumbleweeds. Startled motorists would even veer off the road in order to avoid hitting them.

(Source: Atlas of the Mysterious in North America by Rosemary Ellen Guiley)

Salt Creek:
(Directions: 30 miles N of Casper)
Bright yellow ghost lights have been reported near the Salt Creek Oil Field, 30 miles north of Casper, since the turn of the 20th Century. The lights appear singly, and seem to glide along the outskirts of the field. They change from yellow to golden. The early sheep ranchers, many of whom were from Ireland and Scotland, believed the lights were lanterns carried by the spirits of the dead.

In the 1920s, a popular story was that the lights were the lantern carried by a local resident named O'Rourke, who had died suddenly of a heart attack one night while sitting at the dinner table.

The lights can be viewed from the Shepperson Ranch Road, ten miles west of the oil field. The phenomenon occurs most often on cool, clear nights. They had been repeatedly seen by a school teacher, Billie Jean Beaton, while living on a ranch in the region. They seem to follow the contours of the land.

(Source: Atlas of the Mysterious in North America by Rosemary Ellen Guiley)

INTERNATIONAL SPOOKLIGHTS

AUSTRALIA

Picton:
(Directions: SW of Sydney, near Campbelltown)

Ghost lights have been seen flitting about the east entrance to Mushroom Tunnel, which was in service from 1867 to 1919. Sometimes the lights merge into what has been described as an apparition of a Lady in White.

The ghost is alleged to be that of Emily Bollard, a 53-year-old woman who was killed in the tunnel in 1916. She was taking a shortcut to visit her brother when she was hit by a train about halfway into the tunnel and killed instantly. Mysterious lights have only recently, however, been seen at the entrance to the now abandoned tunnel.

Min Min Light:
(Directions: Queensland)

There is a report of a Min Min light dating back to 1998 near the town of Miles (Western Queensland). The witness was a repair man who worked at retrieving broken down vehicles or fixing them on the side of the road. The sighting occurred on a Tuesday night about 9 p.m. The disabled vehicle that he received a call about was broken down approximately 10 kilometers west of Miles. He had to make a trip back to town to grab some correct size belts for the vehicle. On the way back out of town to the vehicle (He was approximately 1 km from town heading west),when he noticed a light behind him in his rear view mirror, approximately 1 km behind him.

The light stayed the same distance for about 7 km to the top of this hill. Before he went down the slope, the light was still about 1 km away. He thought, at first, it was a motorcycle. When he got to the bottom of the slope (approximately 1km down the track), he noticed the light was right behind him. Nothing on the road could travel that fast. He was very surprised, the light now traveling 10 meters behind him.

This went on for 2 more kms until he pulled off to the side of the road to the broken down vehicle. He pulled in front of the vehicle and got out of his vehicle and saw that the light had stopped 20 meters back on the side of the road. He thought it was still a motorcycle until he looked properly to see it was too big of a light for a bike and also there was nobody behind it. The light illuminated all the surrounding trees.

He described it as being approximately 1 foot in diameter. The people in the broken down vehicle were not able to directly see the light because of his vehicle parked in front. He asked them to come around to the other side and take a look at the "Min Min light" they said, "It's a car coming." He asked them again to come around, so they came around the other side and looked; they were shocked and scared. They said, "What is it?" He told them it was a "Min Min light," as he had seen them before but never this close. It was a husband and wife with the broken down vehicle and they had never heard of these lights before. They were very frightened by it. After they came around the other side of the vehicle the light slowly sank down onto the road. It hovered there for about 10-15 seconds then came back up to the same height of about 3-4 feet in the air. He was completely awestruck by the incident. It was such a fascinating phenomenon to have been able to see. The light hovered for about another 20 seconds then shot back down the road where it came from, lighting the sides of the road as it went. It left with incredible speed. The witness couldn't explain what the light was!! It couldn't have been anything man made. He would say it traveled at approximately 500 km per hr. It was extremely quick.

The color of the light was a pale yellow and extremely bright. When the light was sitting there at the side of the road it looked as though it was checking them out.

BRAZIL

Limeira Lights:
(Directions: located in town of Limeira about 70 miles NW of Campinas in the Sao Paulo state of Brazil)

Strange apparitions and lights have been seen above the Roman Catholic church in the Pires district city of Limeira for many years. In February 1997, a wedding at the church was completely disrupted by a luminous ball of light floating above the church, and photographer Carlos Pancieri was able to videotape five minutes of the light's presence.

The ball of light moves low over rooftops in the area of the church.

(Source: International Directory of Haunted Places by Dennis William Hauck)

CANADA

British Columbia:
(Directions: between Nakusp and Fauguier on Hwy 6 S)
A driver experienced an unusual sighting in June 1999 and he was traveling alone at night. He was heading South on Hwy 6 between Nakusp and Fauquier; there was no traffic. He suddenly saw a small ball of light coming towards him on the other side of the road. It sort of bounced and floated along for a few seconds and then it scooted off into the bushes on the side of the road. The driver slowed down to see if there was a driveway there where it left the road but there was not. It resembled a motorcycle headlight because it was yellow/white. But a bike would not move like this light did.
(Source: International Directory of Haunted Places by Dennis William Hauck)

Manitoba:
(Directions: near Woodridge)
A single light is often seen in a forest near the town of Woodridge.
(Source: Atlas of the Mysterious in North America by Rosemary Ellen Guiley)

Ontario:
(Directions: near Brechin)
A single moving light is seen along the north shore of Lake Simcoe near town. It enjoys playing hide-and-seek with police officers and even halts trains passing by! Engineers stop their trains, climb out to see what the red light is for, and are stunned by a red ball of light that flies into a nearby wooded area.

Buck Hill:
(Directions: Buck Hill is located in the Ottawa Valley about 90 KM from Pembroke and near to Algonquin Park)
Back during the Depression, a family lived on Buck Hill Road. During a harsh winter a man went out to fetch some firewood and upon his return, his wife informed him that the family dog had gotten out and his young daughter had ran after the canine. He grabbed a lantern and desperately searched for his daughter without success. She was never found.
The light that is seen today is supposed to be the father still searching for

his daughter after all of these years. The lights are described as either white, amber or green and approximately the size of a baseball. Occasionally these lights are even bright enough to light up the forested area and will flare up as if increasing in size and luminosity before eventually disappearing.

One eyewitness account relates how they saw a eerie green glow from the valley while they sat in their truck waiting for the light to make an appearance. It was a green light walking down the road, and then out of nowhere it would increase in speed, perhaps as fast as 100 mph! Then it would make a dead stop and go back to its amazingly fast speed quite quickly.

They watched it for about 30 seconds as the light changed from a green to an orange or amber-colored orb and simply wandered off.

London Light:
(Directions: near London on Hwy 401)
This report comes from John Cachel, Patron Member of the *Ghost Research Society* and occurred around Thanksgiving:

"I remember when I left Rochester, New York for Hamilton in Canada to see the professional bodybuilders competitions. After the show, Walter and I left for Chicago for Thanksgiving break. At about 2:00 a.m., Walter took a nap while I drove on Hwy 401 in Ontario.

"The night was dark and clear with few cars at this time of the morning. I noticed something like a ball floating up and down cross the highway. It was about the size as a basketball and as bright as you see Venus in the evening. The light was about 100 to 150 feet from me at the time. I thought that someone holding a flashlight had run across the street but there was nothing under the light! It took about five seconds to cross the highway and when I passed it, I could see the light went into the woods."

Niagara-on-the-Lake Lights:
(Directions: near Niagara-on-the-Lake)
Bright, deep-orange lights were seen frequently in the sky from 1975 to 1980. They moved at high speed and along very erratic paths, sometimes executing 90-degree turns.

(Source: Atlas of the Mysterious in North America by Rosemary Ellen Guiley)

Nova Scotia:
(Directions: Oak Island money pit on in Mahone Bay)
Ghost lights have been seen flitting about this famous "Money Pit", where at least six people lost their lives attempting to retrieve the treasure of long-

dead pirates.

(Source: International Directory of Haunted Places by Dennis William Hauck)

Ghost Road Lights:

(Directions: near Port Perry a suburb of Toronto. Take Ontario Hwy 7 E out of North Toronto about 60 km's to town of Port Perry, pass through town, across Lake Scugog out to the island. The ghost appears in a farmer's field at the bottom of a dirt road, which ends at a T-intersection at one of the concession roads. Go north on the dirt road about 1000 yards from the T-intersection and then turn your car around so that you face south)

In a farmer's field, a ghost of a man killed on a motorcycle haunts an open area that he was riding through when he died. The accident took place in 1976 and was caused when the motorcyclist ran into a barbed wire fence that the rider didn't see. The unfortunate victim was either Dan or Dave Sweeney, according to local legends. The road nearby has acquired the nickname Ghost Road.

Ever since then, witnesses have reported a light, resembling a single light from a motorcycle, coming at them from a distance in the field. As the motorcycle passes by, the red taillight can often be seen as well. The headlight appears to be pure white, not unlike a standard HMI light. It does not throw a beam, and the purity and quality of the light seems to be unaffected by rain, snow, or fog.

As far as ghost appearances go, you can practically set your watch by this one. It can be seen up to 275 nights a year, generally between the hours of 2300h and 0200h. The apparition can appear anywhere from one to ten times a night. Best time of year: The month directly before Halloween, and the month directly after.

(Source: International Directory of Haunted Places by Dennis William Hauck)

Spirit Hill:

(Directions: located on Cape Sable Island and the Centreville Woods)

Lights have been seen here for many years. If you should go down to the South Side on this island around 2 a.m., you might glimpse a light on the beach. Those who have viewed the light say that it resembles a ball of fire that floats through the air. One onlooker attempted to shoot the light, only to have his gun burst on him!

Another individual had the light follow him and his horse and team closely. The faster he drove, the faster the light increased in speed, perfectly

keeping pace with him.
(Source: Bluenose Ghosts by Helen Creighton)

Sudbury:
(Directions: near Sudbury along an old farm road, just on the borders of old Hammer, about 30-35 minutes N of Sudbury in a small valley within the Sudbury Basin known as Valley East)

Reports of a small orb of bright, electric-blue have been seen in the area. These lights have been known to float perhaps seven to eight feet off the ground and sometimes even illuminate the hillside with its glow.

Others have observed a deep, blood-red sphere that slowly gains in brightness until it is no longer visible. It also floats a good eight feet above the ground. It may stay in your field of vision for a bit before slowly melting away! The orbs are about the size of a large grapefruit or softball. The light they shed was similar to plasma or halogen.

Saskatchewan:
(Directions: near Beechy)
A single light is often reported in the Buffalo Basin area of this region.
(Source: Atlas of the Mysterious in North America by Rosemary Ellen Guiley)

Pelican Narrows Lights:
(Directions: light is observed in the Pelican Narrows Reservation)
The cemetery for this reserve, which is located on an island, is haunted. Glowing spheres of light are seen floating in and out of the trees of the island as if they were performing a ceremony or dance ritual. Sometimes the balls, which vary in brightness and size, move at rapid speeds through the woods. At other times the globes of light follow people. The Native Canadians believe the balls of light are the spirits of their dead ancestors.
(Source: International Directory of Haunted Places by Dennis William Hauck)

Saint Louis Ghost Light:
(Directions: light is observed in Saint Louis about 19 miles from Prince Albert)
Near the town is a ghostly light that has been witnessed by dozens of people. The Saint Louis Ghost Light travels down a bumpy gravel road that once was a railroad bed. At first the light appears as if someone is carrying a lantern towards you. It seems to be swinging slightly from a person walking.

According to legend, a railway worker was walking on the tracks with his lamp and was killed when the train backed into him.

(Source: International Directory of Haunted Places by Dennis William Hauck)

CHINA

Bodhisattva Lights:
(Directions: western mountains of China)

The Chinese are extremely into ancestral worship and strong believers of life after death. They believe that the soul can take on many different forms, including that of simple balls of light. In the western mountains of China they even constructed a temple to observe what they called the Bodhisattva Lights, which danced around for many years.

In 1937 a writer, John Blofeld, described the lights from personal experience as such, "fluffy balls of orange-colored fire, moving through space, unhurried and majestic..."

COLOMBIA

Yatacue Bridge:
(Directions: Yatacue is located five miles SW of the town of El Danubio on the Anchicaya River near where it comes together with the Digua River)

The roads in the area are haunted by the phantom of an empty, silent pickup truck that appears out of nowhere and disappears just as mysteriously. Sometimes only the dim yellow headlights of the truck are seen. According to legend, the truck was involved in an accident in early 1970s and went over the bridge, killing a passenger and paralyzing the driver at the same time.

(Source: International Directory of Haunted Places by Dennis William Hauck)

ENGLAND

Avebury:
Orange balls of light were observed by many in 1989 near the great stone

circle of Avebury that quite literally surrounds the entire town.

Castlerigg Run:
Lights similar to the ones at Avebury were spotted around this ancient site around 1919. One observer was quoted as saying, "Whilst we were watching, one of the lights came straight to the spot where we were standing; at first very faint, as it approached the light increased in intensity. When it came close, it slowed down, stopped, quivered and slowly went out."

Congleton:
(Directions: seen near the Bridestones)
Strange lights have been reported near the Neolithic megaliths known as the Bridestones, which is a burial chamber near the town of Congleton.

Lantern Pike:
(Directions: about 10 miles SW of the village of Hayfield)
It is said that a local legend, Peggy wi'th Lantern, was often seen here swinging a lantern at the summit of the hill.

Longdendale Lights:
(Directions: located in the High Peak of Derbyshire)
These lights are sometimes also called the Devil's Bonfires. Some believe that these lights were attributed to the name Shining Clough, one of the mountainous areas that they are often seen at night. Others say they the burning torches of dead Roman soldiers who trek across the lonely moor every night of the first full moon in spring. These lights have been reported for centuries and show no sign of letting up. The lights are usually described as large and pulsating. Sometimes multiple lights are viewed at the same time.

There is a live Webcam of the valley called the "Haunted Valley Webcam" at www.hauntedvalley.com/webcam.htm

Meg o'th Lantern Lane:
(Directions: south of the River Derwent near the town of Derby)
This strange light was often seen on the south side of the river very near town.

Nine Stones Close Circle:
(Directions: located on Harthill Moor)
A eerie blue light is said to emerge from a nearby wooded area and hovers near Nine Stones Close Circle on the moor. Legends abound about the place

being a meeting place for local fairies who would dance and frolic in the area.

River Dove:
(Directions: located at Dovedale in the White Peak)
An eye witness encountered strange lights in 1994, which haunt the valley in this district. The lights apparently dance and bob above the waters of the river at night.

Rushton:
(Directions: on the Staffordshire moors)
A pale blue light is alleged to haunt the hillside near Rushton where the ghost of a murdered woman was buried.

Saxons Lowe:
(Directions: near a farm by Tittensor)
A spook light is supposed to follow a path between a burial mound called Saxons Lowe and a nearby farm.

St. Alban's Light:
A father and son had an encounter with the famous St. Alban's Light September 1999 around 11:30 p.m. They observed two white lights in the night sky, hovering completely silently. The couple surmised that these were actually two weather balloons, or a similar object, and paid no further attention to the skyward lights.

Then something attracted the father's attention; low on the ground, about grass height was a bright glowing, hovering light about the size of a tennis ball. About that same time, the floating lights in the sky came down and merged with the red ball on the ground. After that, they didn't see much more, as they quickly ran from the area.

Stanton Moor:
A large collection of lights have been observed on the moors late at night by motorists.

ITALY

Rome:
(Directions: Pantheon)

Strange balls of blue light and the apparitions of pagan priests have been seen here.

(Source: International Directory of Haunted Places by Dennis William Hauck)

JAPAN

Mt. Senchara:

This story is courtesy of lifetime GRS member and investigator Shinichiro Namiki from Tokyo, Japan:

About 7:30 p.m. on July 31, 1982, Ms. Yoko Yarimizu (thirty-eight-years old at the time), a housewife of Kirihata Yamagata City, Yamagata Prefecture, was surprised to find that there was something like a fire at the top of Mt. Senchara (1,182 meters above sea level) in the east when she went out to the backyard in order to dump garbage.

She informed her family members of the strange sight. When her husband Kazumi (forty-one years old at the time) and other members of the family went outside, there was an orange luminous body, as large as a star of the first magnitude, near the crest line of the mountain although the "ghost light?" had disappeared. The luminous body disappeared in five seconds. Then, it appeared at a mountain side and disappeared again.

This phenomenon happened several times. And then, the two luminous bodies, one was orange and the other was light blue, appeared side by side. These two round luminous bodies disappeared soon after they moved horizontally. The lights repeated their appearances and disappearances several times. The number of the luminous body was, at one time, only one, at another time, was two.

At about 8 p.m., the pressmen of the Yamagata Shinbun and some cameramen rushed to the spot through Kazumi's notification. But, there was no ghost light appearance for some time. Then, at about 9:30 p.m., the crest line of the mountain became bright momentarily and a bluish ghost light appeared.

A cameraman, Nobuyuki Kobayashi, pressed the shutter hurriedly. The ghost light disappeared soon again. Immediately after this, a blue gleam ran across the sky from the crest line of the mountain. This phenomenon was the final stage of a two-hour fuss over the ghost light.

It was cloudy with a gentle wind that night. And the moon's age was 12 days. The moon, three days before its fullness, was lighting the area from behind the clouds. Visibility was good.

NORWAY

Hessdalen:
(Directions: this is a valley in the middle of Norway, in Holtalen, SE of Trondheim, about 30 Km's NW of Roros.)

The strange lights that haunt this valley were first reported in December 1981. Approximately 15-20 reports were cataloged each and every week until the summer of 1984 and in 1996 there were only 17 reports.

The light is huge and takes on different shapes. Observations have lasted over an hour at times in a stationary position or it can also move around in the valley. It has been seen to pulsate and it can even illuminate the ground because of its bright intensity. Colors vary from mostly yellow to red or even blue.

SINGAPORE

Lor Halus:
This sand and storage area of Singapore is known for its population and grime. However, people fishing overnight from piers here often report paranormal phenomena such as strange voices, balls of blue light and apparitions. Check out the Singapore Ghosts Web site at www.cyberway.com.sg/~leo81/main.htm.

(Source: International Directory of Haunted Places by Dennis William Hauck)

SWEDEN

Lake Langhalsen:
In August 1972, Olof Frederiksson noticed a blue-tinged ball of light hovering over the lake, northwest of Nykoping, after the lights in his summer cottage had dimmed. When it disappeared, the lights in his cottage returned to normal.

(Source: Earth Lights Revelation by Paul Devereux)

<u>Navekvarn:</u>
In April 1972, motorist Sven Narholm was followed for over ten minutes by a blue-green ball of light. The light measuring close to a meter wide came to within 11 yards of his car and apparently caused interference on his car radio. The silent orb then flew to a nearby woods and disappeared.
(Source: Earth Lights Revelation by Paul Devereux)

<u>Nykoping/Oxelosund area:</u>
On January 8, 1977, at least 50 eyewitnesses saw five red, glowing discs or balls of light.
(Source: Earth Lights Revelation by Paul Devereux)

WEST AFRICA

<u>Lake Ncovi:</u>
(Directions: between Ogowe and Rembwe rivers, Gabon)
In 1895, Mary Kingsley was on an exploration around Lake Ncovi. She went alone one night to bathe in the waters of the lake when she noticed an unusual phenomenon:

"Down through the forest on the lake bank opposite came a violet ball the size of a small orange. When it reached the sand beach it hovered along it to and fro close to the ground. In a few minutes another ball of similarly colored light came towards it from behind one of the islets, and the two wavered to and fro on the beach, sometimes circling each other. I made off towards them in a canoe, thinking - as I do - they were some brand new kind of luminous insect. When I got onto their beach one of them went off into the bushes and the other away over the water. I followed in the canoe and, when I thought I had almost got it, it went down into the water and I could see it glowing as it sunk until it vanished in the depths."

(Source: Earth Lights Revelation by Paul Devereux)

In Conclusion

As you have read, there are hundreds and hundreds of these spook lights located all around the world. This book does not list all of them by any means. I have tried to resource these lights through books, newspaper articles, videos, personal experiences, interviews of eyewitnesses and, of course, the Internet.

You have probably noticed many similarities and commonalities in these reports such as the location of these lights. Many have been reported along lonely stretches of roadway, alongside lakes or streams and on railroad tracks. These locales are the most often reported places where spook lights have been observed. Local legends often abound in conjunction with these lights such as some kind of untimely death that has taken place at some time in the past. Most often it is an accidental beheading of an individual or railroad employee. Other times there seems to be no logical reason for the appearance of the phenomena.

Sometimes the phenomena stops with the removal of the railroad tracks or paving of a road; other times it just continues as though nothing has been changed or that the change has not affected the light or ghost in any manner.

If you plan to visit any of these sights especially at night, here are some tips for you to remember.

1. Never go alone. It's not the ghost or light that you should be afraid of, it's the common folk in this often remote area. Plus, if your car has a breakdown, you'll be stranded there for quite sometime.

2. Never trespass on private property. If you aren't sure the spook light is on private property, ask neighbors in the area or the local police. You wouldn't want to spend a weekend of your research in the local jail or, worse, a butt full of buckshot from an angry property owner.

3. Visit the area during the daylight first so that you can get a better feel of what the place will look like at night.

4. Bring plenty of flashlights and extra batteries.

5. A CB radio is nice for emergencies but a cellular phone is better.

6. Other equipment, which is almost necessary would be cameras with high-speed film, tripods, compasses, notebook, pencils, maps of the area and binoculars.

7. Never litter! Leave the place as you found it minus candy wrappers, soda cans, film canisters and other garbage. Nothing ruins it for future researchers than to have the local residents angry at the mess you left.

8. Always tell a friend or even a local in town what you are doing and where you will be at any particular time. Sheriffs, librarians or city officials are often willing to help you and sometimes even provide safety if they know you are a serious researcher.

9. Never bring beer or alcoholic beverages to a site and don't smoke while taking pictures or videotaping.

10. Respect the peace of others by keeping your voices in a hushed tone especially if you are near farmhouses or local residences and especially if you are out there in the wee morning hours.

If you abide by these simple rules, it will make your investigation of a spook light flow smoother without any mishaps or problems. And, if you know of any ghost lights that I missed, by all means please write to me at: The Ghost Research Society, PO Box 205, Oak Lawn, IL. 60454-0205 or email me at: dkaczmarek@ghostresearch.org.

I would love to hear from you especially if you capture any strange or unusual images whether they be on photographs or videos. Good hunting!

ACKNOWLEDGEMENTS

There have been many people who gratefully helped in the writing of this book whether it be through pictures, maps, information, websites or allowing me to use some of their written material. I would like to personally thank the following people:

Rosemary Ellen Guiley for allowing me to quote from her book "Atlas of the Mysterious in North America", Shinichiro Namiki from Tokyo for the Japanese ghost light picture, Indianola, Iowa Public Library, John Cachel for the great hand-drawn maps of various ghost light sites and pictures, Randy Liebeck and the Vestigia Project for the information taken from their investigation of the Hookerman Light and the various pictures, Mike Frizzell of the Enigma Project, Dennis William Hauck author of "National Directory of Haunted Places" for allowing me to reprint some of the material from his book, Joplin Public Library, Sarah Judd of Neosho, Missouri for sending me a tape of our appearance on KSN, Jennifer Haile of KSN, Marta Churchwell of the Joplin Globe for pictures of the light, Dina Taylor of the Joplin Museum Complex for the immense amount of written literature provided, Lamar James of the Arkansas Gazette, Troy Taylor author of "Haunted Illinois", various websites on spook lights and to all those who contributed oral stories who either wished to remain anonymous or didn't give their names. Thanks!

And a special thanks to Christina Wallbruch for suggesting the title for this book!

REFERENCES

Alabama:
The National Directory of Haunted Places - Dennis William Hauck, Penguin Books, 1996.

Arizona:
The National Directory of Haunted Places - Dennis William Hauck, Penguin Books, 1996.

Arkansas:
"The Gurdon Light Phenomena: You Must See It To Understand It"- Arkansas Gazette, Nancy Coon Sparks, 6-22-80.
"Ghost Light Focus of Spirited Search"- Arkansas Gazette, Lamar James, 9-10-84.
"Ghost Lights Just One of Life's Mysteries," Gazette Telegraph, Scott Smith.

California:
The National Directory of Haunted Places - Dennis William Hauck, Penguin Books, 1996.

Delaware:
The National Directory of Haunted Places - Dennis William Hauck, Penguin Books, 1996.

Florida:
Atlas of the Mysterious in North America - Rosemary Ellen Guiley, Facts On File, Inc., 1995.
The National Directory of Haunted Places - Dennis William Hauck, Penguin Books, 1996.

Georgia:
"Ghost Light of Screven" - The Atlanta Journal, John Vardeman, 10-29-82.
Savannah Morning News - 10-23-1872.

Illinois:
Ghost Trackers Newsletter - Dale Kaczmarek, Vol. 1, No. 1, Nov. 1982.
Psychic City Chicago - Brad Steiger, Doubleday & Co., Inc. 1976.
"Unwinding the Yarn of Kankakee Folklore" - Kankakee Journal, Lisa Hoss, 8-26-84.
"The Legend of Jacob's Ladder" - Kankakee Journal, Mike Lyons, 10-30-88.
Chicago Magazine - Christopher Hill, Oct. 1988
Haunted Illinois - Troy Taylor, Whitechapel Productions, 1999.

Indiana:
Hoosier Haunts - K.T. MacRorie, Thunder Bay Press, 1997.

Iowa:
The Ghost of St. Mary's - Roy E. Whitehead, Dec. 1952.
Historic Haunted America - ("The Beacon") - Michael Norman & Beth Scott, Tom

Doherty Assc., LLC, 1995.

Kansas:
Haunted Kansas - Lisa Hefner Heitz, University Press of Kansas, 1997.

Michigan:
Laurie Small from the Internet
Ghost Trackers Newsletter - Dale Kaczmarek, Vol. 4, No. 4, Oct. 1985.

Minnesota:
The National Directory of Haunted Places - Dennis William Hauck, Penguin Books, 1996.
Ghosts of the Prairie Website - Troy Taylor, www.prairieghosts.com

Mississippi:
The National Directory of Haunted Places - Dennis William Hauck, Penguin Books, 1996.

Missouri:
Ghost Trackers Newsletter - Dale Kaczmarek, Vol. 2, No. 3, July 1983.
"Town Spooked by Odd Light" - St. Louis Dispatch, John Rogers, 10-25-97.
"Old Faithful of the Ozarks" - Fate Magazine, Wann Smith & William Equels, Oct. 1996.
Atlas of the Mysterious in North America - Rosemary Ellen Guiley, Facts On File, Inc., 1995.
The International Directory of Haunted Places - Dennis William Hauck, Penguin Books, 1996.
"Ozark Spook Light: A Scientific Report" - Raymond Bayless, Fate Magazine, October/November 1964

Nevada:
Mysterious Fires and Lights - Vincent H. Gaddis, David McKay Co., Inc.,1967.

New Jersey:
Atlas of the Mysterious in North America - Rosemary Ellen Guiley, Facts On File, Inc., 1995.

New York:
Atlas of the Mysterious in North America - Rosemary Ellen Guiley, Facts On File, Inc., 1995.

North Carolina:
"Strange Lights Still Seen in Rowan" - The News & Observer, Heath Thomas, 4-11-65.
"Cohoke Light One of Dozens in the Country" - The Tidewater Review, Jeff Byrd, 10-18-78.
"It" - Sunday News Magazine, Douglas Bartholomew, 6-25-78.
"Search Adds To Mystery of Brown Mountain Lights" - 8-3-62.
"A New Ghost Light in North Carolina" - The News & Observer, Harold Black, 2-5-61.

"Strange Light in a Dark Swamp" - The News & Observer, John Coit, 12-7-69.
"Solving the Spook Light Mystery" - UFO Report, Peter Jordan & Rita Allen, 1978.
Atlas of the Mysterious in North America - Rosemary Ellen Guiley, Facts On File, Inc., 1995.
The National Directory of Haunted Places - Dennis William Hauck, Penguin Books, 1996.
Ghost Trackers Newsletter - Dale Kaczmarek, Vol. 3, No. 3, July 1984.
North Dakota:
Atlas of the Mysterious in North America - Rosemary Ellen Guiley, Facts On File, Inc., 1995.

Oklahoma:
Ada Evening News - John Bennett, November 1962
"The Death of the Sand Springs, Oklahoma Ghost Light" - INFO Journal, Paul A. Roales, July 1989.
"Ghost Light at Sand Springs Fades: Teen-Age Pranksters Are Unmasked" - Tulsa World News, 9-28-54.
Atlas of the Mysterious in North America - Rosemary Ellen Guiley, Facts on File, Inc., 1995.

Pennsylvania:
The National Directory of Haunted Places - Dennis William Hauck, Penguin Books, 1996.

South Carolina:
South Carolina Ghosts - Nancy Roberts, University of South Carolina Press, 1983.
Charlotte News - March 1962.

Tennessee:
Haunted Tennessee - Charles Edwin Price, The Overmountain Press, 1995.

Texas:
Houston Chronicle Magazine - Mike Blakely, 8-31-86.
Ford Times - Leslie Rich, Vol. 56, No. 10, Oct. 1963.
Skeptical Inquirer - Herbert Lindee, Vol. 16, Summer 1992.
The National Geographic - Oct. 1974.
The National Directory of Haunted Places - Dennis William Hauck, Penguin Books, 1996.
Atlas of the Mysterious in North America - Rosemary Ellen Guiley, Facts On File, Inc., 1995.
Mysterious America - Loren Coleman, Faber & Faber, Inc., 1983.

Vermont:
The National Directory of Haunted Places - Dennis William Hauck, Penguin Books, 1996.

Virginia:
Atlas of the Mysterious in North America - Rosemary Ellen Guiley, Facts on File, Inc., 1995.

Mysterious Fires and Lights - Vincent H. Gaddis, David McKay Co., Inc., 1967.

Washington:
Atlas of the Mysterious in North America - Rosemary Ellen Guiley, Facts On File, Inc., 1995.
The National Directory of Haunted Places - Dennis William Hauck, Penguin Books, 1996.

West Virginia:
The National Directory of Haunted Places - Dennis William Hauck, Penguin Books, 1996.
Wyoming:
Atlas of the Mysterious in North America - Rosemary Ellen Guiley, Facts on File, Inc., 1995.
Ghosts of the Range: Eerie True Tales of Wyoming - Debra D. Munn, Pruett Publishing Co., 1989.

International Spooklights

Brazil:
The International Directory of Haunted Places - Dennis William Hauck, Penguin Books, 2000.

Canada:

British Columbia:
The International Directory of Haunted Places - Dennis William Hauck, Penguin Books, 2000.
Manitoba:
Atlas of the Mysterious in North America - Rosemary Ellen Guiley, Facts On File, Inc., 1995.

London:
John Cachel, Patron Member of the Ghost Research Society,
http://pages.prodigy.net/ghostfish
Nova Scotia:
The International Directory of Haunted Places - Dennis William Hauck, Penguin Books, 2000.

Niagara-on-Lake:
Atlas of the Mysterious in North America - Rosemary Ellen Guiley, Facts On File, Inc., 1995.

Port Perry:
The International Directory of Haunted Places - Dennis William Hauck, Penguin Books, 2000.

Saskatchewan:
Atlas of the Mysterious in North America - Rosemary Ellen Guiley, Facts On File, Inc., 1995.
The International Directory of Haunted Places - Dennis William Hauck, Penguin Books, 2000.
Bluenose Ghosts - Helen Creighton, McGraw-Hill Ryerson LTD., 1957.

Columbia:
The International Directory of Haunted Places - Dennis William Hauck, Penguin Books, 2000.

Italy:
The International Directory of Haunted Places - Dennis William Hauck, Penguin Books, 2000.

Japan:
Shinichiro Namiki, Japan Space Phenomena Society, Tokyo, Japan.

Singapore:
The International Directory of Haunted Places - Dennis William Hauck, Penguin Books, 2000.

Sweden:
Earth Lights Revelation - Paul Devereux, Blandford Press, 1989.

West Africa:
Earth Lights Revelation - Paul Devereux, Blandford Press, 1989.

Note: Although Whitechapel Productions Press, Dale Kaczmarek, and all affiliated with this book have carefully researched all sources to insure the accuracy of the information contained in this book, we assume no responsibility for errors, inaccuracies or omissions.

Recommended Further Reading

Atlas of the Mysterious in North America - Rosemary Ellen Guiley, Facts On File, Inc., 1995, ISBN: 0-8160-2876-1, www.visionaryliving.com

Curious Encounters: Phantom Trains, Spooky Spots, and Other Mysterious Wonders - Loren Coleman, Faber & Faber, 1985, ISBN: 0-571-12542-5, www.lorencoleman.com

Earth Lights Revelation - Paul Devereux, Blandford Press, 1989, ISBN: 0-7137-2029-8, www.acemake.com/PaulDevereux/earthlights.html

Haunted Illinois - Troy Taylor, Whitechapel Productions, 1999, ISBN: 1-892523-01-9, www.prairieghosts.com

The International Directory of Haunted Places - Dennis William Hauck, Penguin Books, 2000, ISBN: 0-14-029635-2), www.haunted-places.com

The Light at the End of the Road (video) Ted Phillips & John Carpenter, 4033 S. Belvedere, Springfield, MO. 65807, $32.95 (includes shipping)

Lightnings, Auroras, Nocturnal Lights and Related Luminous Phenomena - William R. Corliss, The Sourcebook Project, 1982, ISBN: 0-915554-7, www.science-frontiers.com/sourcebk.htm

The Marfa Lights: A Viewers Guide - Dennis Stacey, 1989.

Mysterious America - Loren Coleman, Faber & Faber, 1983, ISBN: 0-571-12524-7, www.lorencoleman.com

Mysterious Fires and Lights - Vincent H. Gaddis, David McKay Co., Inc., 1967, Library of Congress Catalog Card # 67-16939, www.borderlands.com/catalog/gaddis.htm

The National Directory of Haunted Places - Dennis William Hauck, Penguin Books, 1996, ISBN: 0-14-025734-9, www.haunted-places.com

Ozark Spooklight - Foster Young, Young Publications.

Spookville's Ghost Lights - Bob Loftin

<u>Websites</u>
American Ghost Society
www.prairieghosts.com

Anomalous Luminous Phenomena
www.tuvpo.com/alp/deprem2e.html

Earth Lights & UFOs
www.acemake.com/PaulDevereux/earthlights.html

Enigma Project
http://umbc7.umbc.edu/~frizzell/tep.html

Ghost Lights
www.bigbendquarterly.com/marfa.htm

Ghost Research Society
www.ghostresearch.org

Longdendale Lights Webcam
www.hauntedvalley.com/webcam.htm

Marfa Light
www.marfalights.com

Mystery Lights
www.mysterylights.com

Obiwan's Ghostlight Page
www.ghosts.org

Peakland Spooklights
www.indigogroup.co.uk/edge/Peakland.htm

Spooklight
http://members.tripod.com/~CelticCaper

Vestigia
http://vestigia.iwarp.com

ABOUT THE AUTHOR : DALE KACZMAREK

Dale Kaczmarek is the President of the Ghost Research Society, an international organization of ghost researchers that is based in the Chicago area. He is also the author of WINDY CITY GHOSTS (the original book) and the editor of a number of publications about ghosts and haunting. Dale has also contributed to and appeared in a number of occult-related books, including *Dead Zones* by Sharon Jarvis, The *Encyclopedia of Ghosts and Spirits* by Rosemary Ellen Guiley, *More Haunted Houses* by Joan Bingham and Dolores Riccio, *Haunted Places: The National Directory* by Dennis William Hauck, *Sightings* by Susan Michaels and many others.

Dale has made a number of television appearances on local and national news programs and has appeared in many documentaries and shows about ghosts and hauntings places, including Real Ghost Busters, Sightings, Encounters, The Other Side, Mysteries, Magic & Miracles, A.M. Chicago (with Oprah Winfrey) and many others. He has also appeared on dozens of radio programs and shows as well.

In addition to serving as president of the Ghost Research Society, Dale is also a member of the American Association Electronic Voice Phenomena (AA-EVP), International Fortean Organization (INFO), Society for the Investigation of the Unexplained and an Honorary Member of both the Ghost Club and the American Ghost Society.

He is also the host of the highly recommended Excursions into the Unknown Tours of the Chicagoland Region. He currently resides in the south suburbs of Chicago.

Printed in the United States
73613LV00006B/268-306